Artful CHRISTMAS

Artful CHRISTMAS

30 Elegant Craft Projects

By SUSAN WASINGER

LARK

An Imprint of Sterling Publishing
387 Park Avenue South
New York, NY 10016

Text, illustrations, and photography © 2014 Susan Wasinger

ISBN 978-1-4547-0808-7

Library of Congress Cataloging-in-Publication Data

Wasinger, Susan.
  Artful Christmas / Susan Wasinger.
    pages cm
  Includes index.
  ISBN 978-1-4547-0808-7
  1. Christmas decorations. 2. Handicraft. I. Title.
  TT900.C4.W38 2014
  745.594'12--dc23

2013043162

Distributed in Canada by Sterling Publishing
c/o Canadian Manda Group, 165 Dufferin Street
Toronto, Ontario, Canada M6K 3H6
Distributed in the United Kingdom by GMC Distribution Services
Castle Place, 166 High Street, Lewes, East Sussex, England BN7 1XU
Distributed in Australia by Capricorn Link (Australia) Pty. Ltd.
P.O. Box 704, Windsor, NSW 2756, Australia

For information about custom editions, special sales, and premium and corporate purchases, please contact Sterling Special Sales at 800-805-5489 or specialsales@sterlingpublishing.com.

Email academic@larkbooks.com for information about desk and examination copies. The complete policy can be found at larkcrafts.com.

Every effort has been made to ensure that all the information in this book is accurate. However, due to differing conditions, tools, and individual skills, the publisher cannot be responsible for any injuries, losses, and other damages that may result from the use of the information in this book.

Manufactured in China

2 4 6 8 10 9 7 5 3 1

larkcrafts.com

Life is short, the winter is long, Christmas comes but once a year...

All these things conspire to make our holiday traditions

particularly precious.

How lucky we are to take these darkest days of December

and transform them into a celebration of light.

This will be the first Christmas of my life

without my beloved dad.

You will be missed, Ronald E. Harris.

But we will celebrate you up here on this Colorado

mountainside, and you will forever be a part

of my every season of joy...

Table OF Contents

Techniques–How It's Done **8**

Materials And Tools **11**

Doily Snowflake Bowl **12**

Plaster Relief Ornaments **15**

Pressed Clay Wreath **20**

Toy Catalog Vintage Glitter Garland **22**

Faux Fortuny Chargers **26**

Stenciled Chargers **30**

Marbled Ornaments **34**

Stockings With All The Trimmings **38**

Playing Card Ornaments **43**

Modern Graphic Felted Ornaments **48**

Christmas Beasts For Your Tree **52**

Soda Can Punched Metal Trees **56**

Lacy Stars For Holiday Windows **61**

Wrapping Ideas From The Casbah **66**

Button & String Bows **68**

Bead Emboldened Elizabethan Wreath **70**

Folk Art Felted Coasters **74**

Wool On Linen Table Runner **78**

Folded Page Snowflakes **82**

Glittering Castle **86**

Tiny Tin Advent Calendar Wreath **92**

Cookie Cutter Garland **95**

Snipped Paper Cards **98**

Muslin Bag Advent Calender **102**

Sand Painted Ornaments **106**

Silvered Glass Votive Holders **110**

Color-Blocked Gift Bags **114**

Double Circle Wreath **118**

Folded Star Ornaments **122**

Templates **126**

About the Author **128**

Index **128**

Techniques

HOW IT'S DONE

The holidays are here! No doubt about it, the season of joy is also the busiest part of the year. Most of us hustle to complete the items on lengthy to-do lists: planning parties, buying gifts, checking in with friends and family. But celebrating shouldn't seem like a chore! If holiday preparations have left you feeling more like Scrooge than Santa, then you've come to the right place. Featuring fun, festive projects that can easily be squeezed into a busy schedule, this book is jam-packed with fresh ways you can spiff up your home for the

holidays. The best part: craft expertise isn't required. Many of these projects are short and sweet, made up of easy individual steps. The more involved ones are accompanied by how-to photos that walk you through every part of the process.

Take some time to peruse the jolly projects on the pages that follow, and start with one that speaks to you. Remember—skill is over-rated. In the spirit of the season, this book asks only that you be susceptible to joy and ready to play.

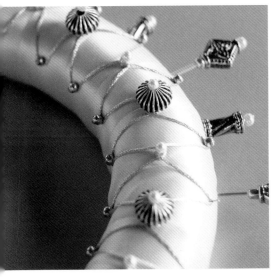

crowd—although he did have a British accent and purple
draped around his neck. "You're Pen, yes? Lovely to see y
And you are?"

"I'm Dice."

"Oh, very nice." Duck tickled us both with his pluma
"Look here, I'm a terribl to get yourselves somethin
He waved an arm to the carts boarded. "Tell me, have
seen my brother? Prob somewhere in the pantry. A
we're supposed to play I took off, in pur
of the feckless Cran

Pen and I mingled, cobbling silence. The Willi
parents must be cool with minor drinking. Very continenta
them. Mm, champagne—my pleasure. We sipped, we nibb
we laughed at the peacocks on the lawn, honking and har
ing the guests. We talked about Kurt Libo, who cleans
okay, wanted to know if they had climbed any trees lately.
had a friend with him, who was being flirty. I placated him
something to do.

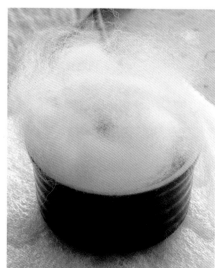

Materials and Tools

Each project in this book begins with a list of necessities. Most of them are available at your neighborhood craft or hardware store, and you may already have some of them in a junk drawer, on a kitchen shelf, or in your recycling bin. Because the holidays can be complicated, I tried to keep the activities in this book simple and stress-free. Each of these projects can be done quicker than you can say Santa Claus. They don't require a great deal of planning. Crafters of all skill levels can easily put them together.

A few of the projects require specialty tools—items that do specific things ever-so-well. The needle-felting tool, for instance, is one such item. It does nothing but jab wool fibers into a glorious tangle to make luscious, soft felt, but five projects in this book use it. The elaborate punches required to create the Soda Can Punched Metal Trees are also used to make unique wrapping solutions for your holiday packages. And glass glitter finds lots of places to sparkle and shine.

Ideas and inspiration without any inconvenience—that's what I hope to provide with this book. Read on, and you'll find out just how easy it is to add a bit of homemade splendor to your holiday—and to make crafting a pleasurable part of the season.

DOILY
Snowflake Bowl

This delicate, lacy bowl is like a snowflake brought inside and magically kept from melting. Created from vintage doilies, it makes a beautiful centerpiece for a holiday table. Use a wax or LED candle to illuminate the filligree.

MATERIALS

white glue

small to medium-sized balloon

vintage crocheted doily
(I used a 9-inch doily)
(22.9 cm)

spray polyurethane
(optional)

TOOLS

disposable bowl for mixing glue

cup or small bowl

paintbrush

PREPARATION: Mix one part white glue with one part water. Blow up the balloon so that it's about the size of a large cantaloupe. Set it on the cup or small bowl to keep it steady.

1 Drape the doily over the balloon and smooth it down over the sides. Make sure the doily drapes evenly over the balloon with no rolled edges or crimped areas. (photo A)

2 Paint the entire surface of the doily liberally with the glue mixture, making sure you work glue into all of the nooks, crannies, and fibers. Make sure no errant blobs of glue remain on the doily. (photo B)

3 Let the doily bowl dry overnight or longer until it's totally stiff. If it isn't stiff, paint it with another layer of glue. When it's completely dry, gently wriggle your fingers beneath it, depressing the balloon. Loosen the doily carefully. Don't puncture the balloon! If you do, the doily bowl will collapse. (photo C)

4 If desired, spray the bowl with polyurethane for added rigidity. Use the bowl as a decorative element or add a candle to make a stunning votive. (photo D)

Plaster Relief

ORNAMENTS

The sumptuous, slightly decadent texture of these sculptural ornaments defies their humble origins. Reminiscent of the intricate carved plasterwork seen in mansions and castles of old, the ornaments are made by pressing pieces of decorative hardware or other household geegaws into crafting clay. It's an easy technique that makes a posh impression.

You'll be surprised at how easily you can find worked and carved designs around the house. Take a little piece of clay with you as you search for patterns, and make test impressions to see what works. Try ornate silver flatware, doorknobs, escutcheons, the scrollwork on antique pieces, and carved moldings or panels. And don't worry—making an impression of an object won't hurt it.

MATERIALS
air-dry clay or
bakeable polymer clay

ribbon for hanging

beeswax
(optional)

TOOLS
rolling pin

household items with
carving or scrollwork
(see opposite)

knife or craft blade

skewer or toothpick

drying rack or
baking sheet

CLOCKWISE FROM TOP LEFT:
Scrollwork and hardware on
an old humpback chest, the
handle of a chafing dish, a
silver service lid, a carved
wooden panel from India,
various pieces of antique
door and cabinet hardware,
pieces of silver flatware.

1 Roll the clay out into thin pancakes about ¼ to ⅜-inch (6 mm to 1 cm) thick. Each pancake should be big enough to cover the object you're making an impression of with an inch (2.5 cm) or so of overhang on all sides. (photo A)

2 To get a complete impression, press the object evenly into the clay. You may need to turn the object over and gently press the back of the clay onto its surface. Don't press too hard or you may go through the clay. (photo B)

3 Gently peel the clay piece off the surface of the object, taking care not to stretch the image. If the impression didn't turn out well, just ball up the clay, roll it out, and try again. If you like the impression, use a knife or craft blade to cut around the outside edge of the design to make an appealing shape. (photo C)

4 Use the skewer or toothpick to poke a hole in the top of the ornament. The hole should be big enough to thread your ribbon through. (photo D)

5 If you're using air-dry clay, place the ornament on a rack and let it dry until it becomes hard. If you're using polymer clay, bake the ornament according to the manufacturer's instructions. (photo E)

NOTE: For added depth and a little hint of tone, rub beeswax across the surface of the dried/baked ornament. Make sure you work the beeswax into the crevices of the piece. Then buff the ornament gently with a cloth.

E

A beautiful alternative to traditional ribbon, these ornaments make extra-festive package toppers.

Pressed Clay
WREATH

1 Roll the clay out into thin pancakes about ¼ inch (6 mm) thick. Each pancake should be large enough to cover the pie server with about a ½ inch (1.3 cm) of overhang all the way around.

2 To get a complete impression, press the pie server evenly into the clay. Cut an even border around the impression with a knife.

3 Gently drape the clay pieces over the foam wreath. Wrap each piece around the underside, and press it into place. If you need more clay in order to wrap the wreath completely, remake the impression and cut it so that there's extra clay at the top and bottom of the impression. Then make another impression and overlap it slightly with the first, draping, wrapping, and pressing it into place. Continue adding pieces until the entire wreath is covered. Let it dry overnight.

4 The clay will shrink a little and slip against the foam form as it dries. To attach each clay piece to the foam and to its neighboring piece, turn the wreath over and apply hot glue to each piece. Then add a ribbon for hanging.

NOTE: Once the wreath is complete, you can enjoy it au naturel, rub it with beeswax, or spray it with protective finish.

MATERIALS

air-dry clay in white or natural

small foam wreath form

ribbon for hanging

beeswax or protective spray finish (optional)

TOOLS

rolling pin

scrollwork pie server

knife or craft blade

hot-glue gun

Pressed, air-dry clay is put to festive use in this everlasting wreath. An antique silver pie server supplies the pretty relief. The finished product resembles a heavily wrought, precious antique. Doesn't much look like a crafty project you can whip up on a weeknight for less than $10, but isn't that the way we like it?

Toy Catalog

VINTAGE

GLITTER GARLAND

Christmas is a holiday of nostalgia and reminiscence, and those qualities inspired this easy-as-pie project. Everything about this vintage garland evokes the past—pages from an old book, illustrations from a classic toy catalog, a gentle dusting of retro sparkle. The glass glitter used here is easy to work with and fun to sprinkle. Just like fairy dust, it'll magically light up any image for the holidays.

MATERIALS

old toy catalog illustrations (see templates page 127)

old book (paperback or hardcover)

white glue and glue stick

glass glitter in a variety of colors

binder hole reinforcement labels

kraft paper scraps

1 yard (.9 m) of ribbon, ¼-inch (6 mm) wide

baker's twine in red and white

TOOLS

color photocopier (or scanner and printer)

straight pin and toothpick

hole punch

PREPARATION: Copy or scan the template images on page 127, enlarging them as needed to fit your book pages. Gently tear or cut pages out of the old book and load them into the paper slot of your copier. Follow the manufacturer's instructions to print the template images onto your book pages. Print each illustration twice so that you can make an eight-foot (2.4 m) garland.

1 Use a straight pin or toothpick to outline parts of each letter in the Christmas greeting with glue. Draw a fine line of glue down one side of each letter as shown. Do as many letters as you can before the glue loses its tack. (photo A)

2 Sprinkle the glitter over the surface of the letters and the glue. Jiggle it around so that it makes contact with all of the glue. (photo B) Dump the excess glitter onto a piece of paper with a crease down the middle. The crease will make it easy to funnel the leftover glitter back into its container for later use.

3 The letters should now have a "drop shadow" of glitter (photo C). Add more glue lines opposite the shadow side as highlights. Sprinkle silver glitter over the letters and shake off the excess.

4 Add color and sparkle to other parts of the illustration. Dab glue in the places where you want extra embellishment, and dust them with colored glitter. Let the illustration dry flat. (photo D)

If you find it hard to draw the glue lines with the pin and the toothpick, try a fine-point glue pen. You can find one at your local craft store. Glue pens are available in a variety of tip widths, and they can make quick work of a job like this.

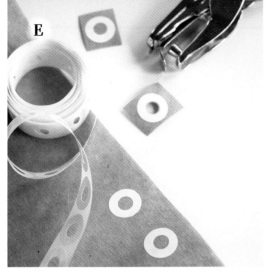

E

F

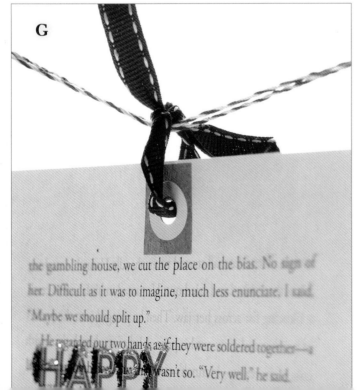

G

H

5 Put binder-hole reinforcement labels on a scrap of kraft paper to create holes for hanging the pages. (photo E)

6 Cut the paper around each label into small rectangles measuring about ¾ x 1 inch (1.9 x 2.5 cm). Glue each kraft sticker into place at the top center of each glittered page. Use a hole punch to make a hole through the paper. (photo F)

7 Thread a 5-inch (12.7 cm) piece of ribbon through the hanging hole, and knot it. Knot the ribbon over a double run of baker's twine to make your garland. The ribbon can be knotted loosely as shown or cinched tightly if you don't want your garland pages to move along the hanging twine. (photo G)

NOTE: The addition of glue and glitter to the pages can make them curl. This is easily fixed by rolling the pages in the opposite direction from the curl and pinning them with clothespins or paper clips. The curl should relax within an hour or so. (photo H)

Faux Fortuny
CHARGERS

To achieve the Fortuny-fabric look that makes this project so sophisticated, use metallic tissue paper with a baroque, old-world pattern. Colored tissue paper will give the charger jewel-toned hues and a classic crinkled effect. The clear glass chargers that complete each setting can be round or square, but they should be ample enough to create a significant border around each dinner plate.

MATERIALS

large glass chargers or circular or
square plates, each 14 inches
(35.6 cm) in diameter

decoupage adhesive medium
(like Mod Podge®)

gold or silver metallic tissue paper

colored tissue paper

TOOLS

paint brush

paper towel or cloth rag

sharp craft knife

A

B

C

D

E

1 Paint the back of one of the glass chargers with the decoupage medium. (photo A)

2 Lay one layer of the gold metallic tissue paper facedown in the wet adhesive on the back of the charger. With a folded paper towel or cloth, smooth the paper into place and gently press out the wrinkles and bubbles. (photo B)

3 Once the tissue and the adhesive are dry, carefully cut around the outside edge of the charger with a sharp craft blade to remove the excess tissue. If there's a bit of overhang, or if the edge gets ragged in places, brush a little adhesive around the edge to smooth it down. (photo C)

4 Gently brush another layer of the decoupage adhesive over the dried metallic tissue on the back of the charger. (photo D)

5 Put a piece of the colored tissue paper on the back of the charger, and press and smooth it down like you did in step 2. Once the tissue is dry, trim around the edge of the charger with the craft blade like you did

in step 3. Add another coat of the decoupage medium to create a more durable surface. (photo E)

NOTE: These chargers are meant to serve as decorative underpinnings for your dinner plates. They aren't meant to hold food. You should wipe them clean instead of submerging them in water.

Stenciled Chargers

These hand-stenciled chargers strike
a pretty balance between whimsy and
grace. The classic, easy-to-execute design
will lend a seasonal touch to your table.

MATERIALS

square plastic chargers with
silver or gold finish

red and/or white craft paint

white, silver, and/or gold
dimensional paint

clear spray finish (optional)

TOOLS

classic geometric stencil
template

masking tape

pounce or stencil brush

1 Position the stencil template on a corner of one of the chargers, and secure it with masking tape. Dip the pounce or stencil brush lightly in the craft paint, and jab it down on the stencil so that the paint goes into the cutaways of the pattern. Go over the stencil multiple times to work paint into all of the areas. The brush works best if you don't angle it. Jab it straight up and down, so that the paint doesn't slide under the edge of the template and blur the pattern's lines. (photo A)

2 When the stencil's paint is thoroughly dry, add dots of dimensional paint using the tip of the paint tube. Outline the pattern with raised dots. For extra texture and visual interest, add a few dots to the center of the stenciled design. (photo B)

3 Once the first group of dots is dry, consider adding more dots in a contrasting color over the stenciled areas. A few dots of silvery dimensional paint will bring a lot of vitality to the simple design. (photo C)

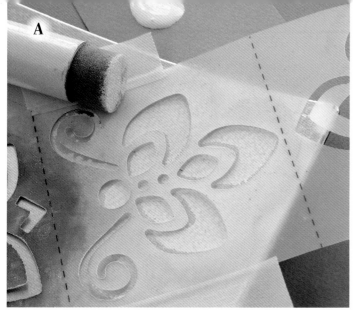

A

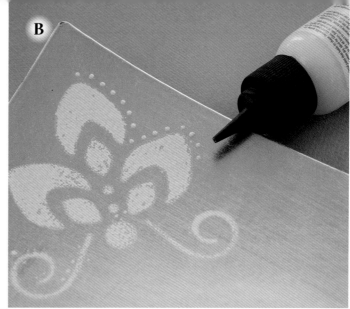

B

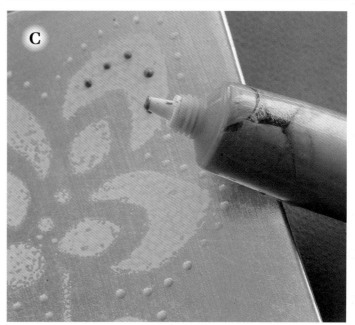

C

The white designs with drops of silver make a delicate and frosty holiday charger. For a little more color, stencil the design in deep red and add dots of white. After the paint has dried, consider safeguarding the design with a coat of spray finish. These chargers are meant to serve as decorative underpinnings for your dinner plates and shouldn't come in direct contact with food. You should wipe them clean instead of submerging them in water.

Marbled
ORNAMENTS

Turn plain-Jane ornaments from the craft store into something special with this easy project. The materials used are newfangled, but the technique draws on marbling methods that were popular in Renaissance Italy.

A

B

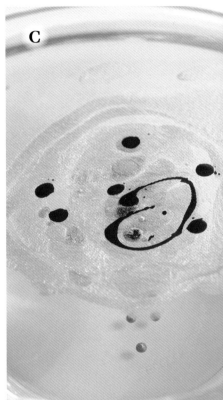

C

D

E

PREPARATION: You'll need a a way to hang the ornament while it dries. I hung mine using a length of string and a bent paper clip.

1 Fill the bowl with water almost to the brim. (photo A)

2 Drip one color of nail polish onto the surface of the water. You can add it in drops or as a ribbon that falls in a swirling pattern. (photo B)

3 Add drops of a second bright color on top of the other polish. You can add drops of other colors if you want, but keep in mind that using more than four different shades can be messy and result in a muddy-looking liquid. (photo C)

4 Drag the tip of the skewer gently across the surface of the liquid so that it pulls the colored polish into an interesting design. Don't swirl the liquid too fast, or the colors will mix too much, and you won't get any cool patterns. (photo D)

5 Remove the wire loop cap from the neck of the ornament. Grasp the ornament firmly with the needle-nosed pliers and, starting at one end of the bowl or tub, gently roll it through the nail polish. Make sure the ornament stays close to the surface. Lift the ornament out of the water and set it down on its back, where there's no polish. Repeat steps 1 through 4, then roll the backside of the ornament across the surface of the liquid to pick up the polish. (photo E) Replace the loop cap and hang the ornament up to dry.

STOCKINGS WITH
All the Trimmings

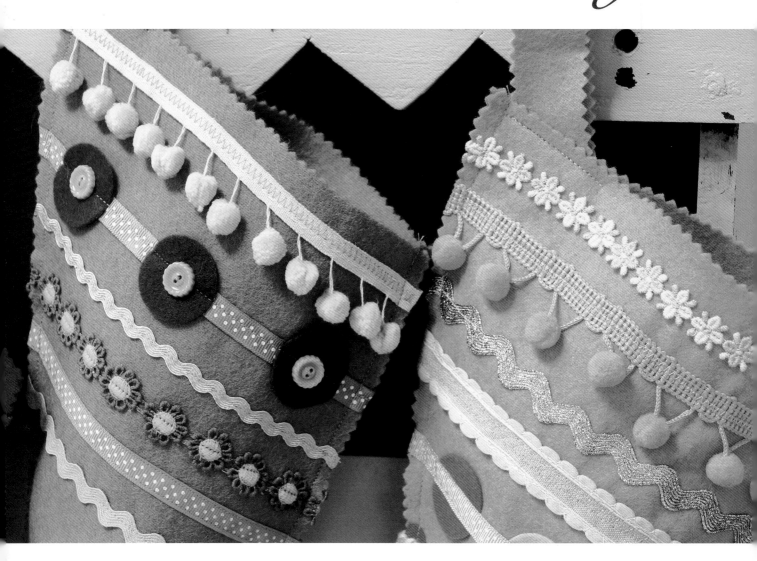

There's something special about the trim aisle of a fabric store—it feels like Christmas there all year 'round. I gathered every festive confection the aisle had to offer to make this project, but I narrowed my palette to one color family per stocking. Basic sewing skills are all you need to create a stocking that's full of fun even when it's empty.

MATERIALS

stocking template, page 128

repositionable glue or
double-stick tape

½ yard (.5 m) of felt for each stocking
(use wool felt or a wool/rayon blend)

¼ yard (.25 m) each of various
trims and ribbons
(6 or 7 different ones per stocking)

temporary glue (optional)

transparent tape

contrasting felt circles or
scraps of felt

assorted buttons

TOOLS

scissors or pinking shears

pins

sewing machine

needle and thread

PREPARATION: Scan and enlarge the stocking template on page 128. Print it out on an 11 x 17-inch (43.2 cm) sheet, and then cut on the line to create the stocking pattern.

1 Using the repositionable glue or the double-stick tape, adhere the stocking template to the felt. Then cut around the outside edge with the pinking shears. Repeat to make a second piece. (photo A)

2 Now it's time to play. Position your trims and ribbons on the stocking, making sure they're parallel to the top edge. Cut each piece so that it's long enough to overhang both sides of the stocking by an inch (2.5 cm) or so. (photo B)

3 Using the repositionable glue or the pins, secure the ribbons in position on the stocking front. Then sew them into place using the sewing machine. If you go slowly, you'll find that the sewing is surprisingly easy. (photo C)

4 Once all of your trims and embellishments are in place, wrap the excess trim ends around to the backside of the stocking front and secure them with a bit of transparent tape. Place the tape far in and away from the edge where you'll be sewing. (photo D)

5 Secure the front and back of the stocking with pins, wrong sides together. Then sew around the perimeter of the stocking about ¼ inch (6 mm) in from the edge (obviously, you'll need to leave the top edge open!). Once the stocking has been sewn, remove the tape pieces on the inside. (photo E)

6 Using the pinking shears, cut a piece of felt that's about ¾ x 8 inches (1.9 x 20.3 cm). Fold the piece in half and tuck the ends into the upper corner of the stocking so that at least half an inch (1.3 cm) is inside the stocking. Sew all four layers of the tab and the stocking two times, about ¼ inch (6 mm) from the top, to secure the hanging tab in place. (photo F)

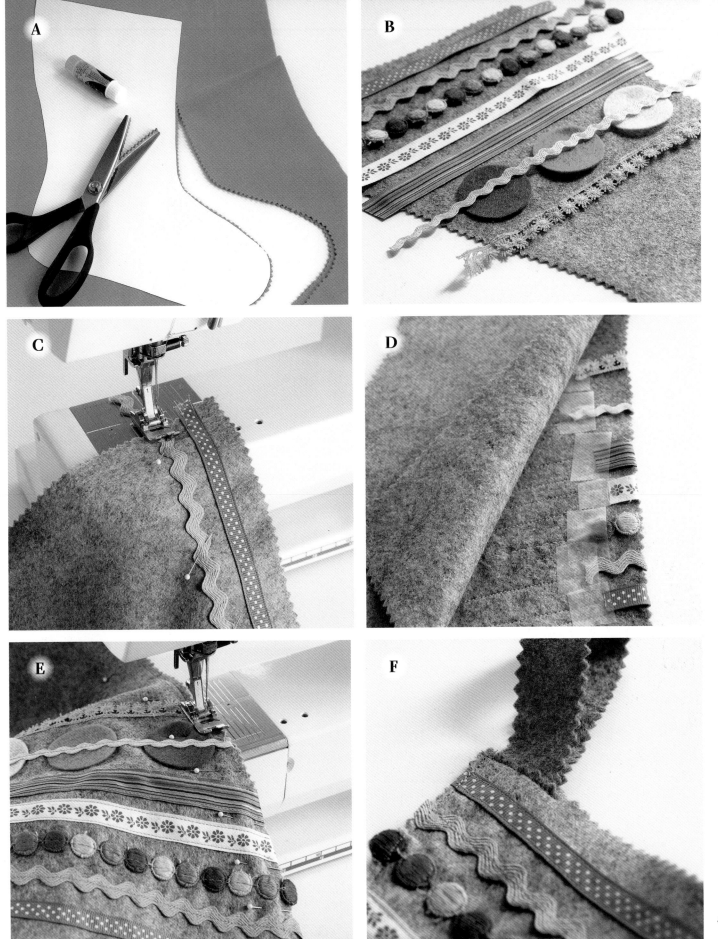

Playing Card ORNAMENTS

This holiday card trick hits the jackpot. With a bit of clever folding, cutting, and gluing, you can transform a humble deck of cards into a group of beautiful, three-dimensional ornaments. Featuring background graphics in rich Christmas red, these decorations are unexpectedly sophisticated.

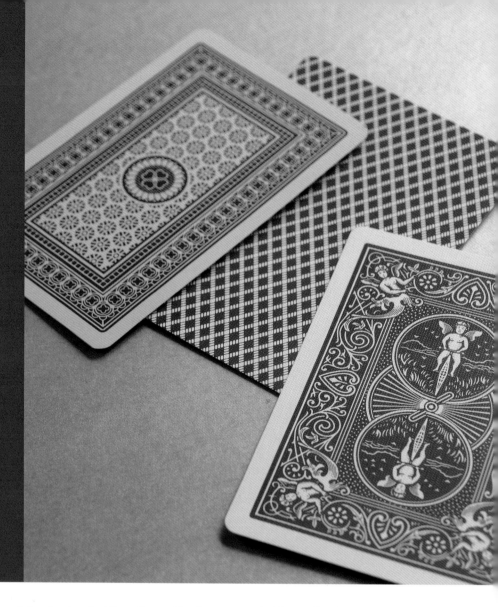

MATERIALS

decks of paper or plastic
playing cards in red

a bit of 18-gauge craft wire

TOOLS

craft punches for cutting out
scalloped squares and circles

bone folder or
butterknife for scoring

straightedged ruler

glue gun

needle-nosed pliers

scissors

PREPARATION: Gather playing cards in a variety of red-and-white patterns. The famous angel-riding-a-bicycle deck is a must-have, but stacks with a simple diamond pattern or alternating borders make lovely additions to the mix.

1 Use the punches to cut out scalloped pieces from the playing cards. You'll need 6 to 8 pieces to make a nice ornament. (photo A)

2 Use the ruler and the bone folder to score the card pieces for folding. To make an ornament from the scalloped squares, fold the pieces on the diagonal. The scalloped ovals can be folded in half the long way. Fold all of the pieces so that the design you want to show on the finished ornament is on the inside of the fold. (photo B)

3 Use the glue gun to apply adhesive to the wrong side of the first card piece. Align one side of another card piece to the first piece, lining up the scalloped edges as best you can. Remember to glue the wrong sides together. Squeeze the pieces together between your thumb and forefinger for a few seconds so that the glue can begin to set. Then add the next folded piece, working around the center until you've used all of your pieces. Do not glue the faces of the last two pieces together because you first need to add a wire hanger (as explained in steps 4 and 5). (photo C)

4 With the needle-nosed pliers, cut a short length of the craft wire (about 2½ inches [6.4 cm]). Twist the wire with the tip of the pliers to form a tiny hanging loop on one end. (photo D)

5 Place the wire in the spine of the glued card pieces. Run the glue gun up and down the wire, making sure to get plenty of glue into the crack. Then add hot glue to the two remaining unglued surfaces of the card ornament. (photo E)

6 Fold and squeeze the last two faces of the card together around the hanging wire and hold them in place until set. Your ornament is now ready to hang. (photo F)

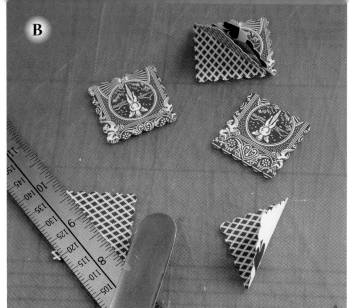

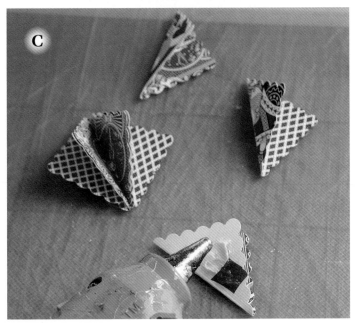

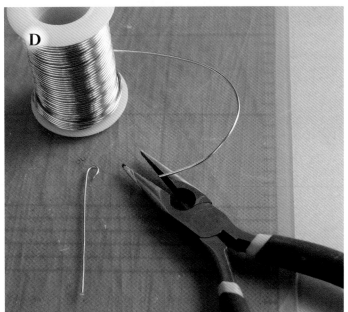

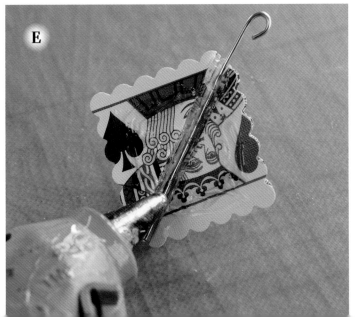

45

Additional How-to

The basic technique of folding and gluing card pieces together around a central axis can be used to create many different types of ornaments. Add some extra cuts with the scissors, and things get even more interesting! Here are three great ornament variations:

#1 This triple decker ornament is composed of a folded-in-half, scalloped-edge oval ornament, which forms the top. Then comes a spindly section made from strips of cards cut the long way, folded in half, and glued together as shown. The bottom section uses full cards folded in half the long way and glued together. They're then cut with scissors so that they come to a point in the center. Finally, they're trimmed back to the base at the top and bottom as shown.

#2 This ornament is made from cards folded in half the short way. Once the cards are glued together, their white border is cut away on a diagonal. A triangular notch is then cut out of each card, giving the ornament a star-like profile.

#3 This ornament looks more complex than it really is. It's composed of cards folded diagonally, but the pieces alternate between being folded from top left to bottom right and top right to bottom left. This alternating orientation gives the finished ornament its fluted profile. Once all of the pieces are folded and glued together, the white border is cut off with scissors.

Modern Graphic
FELTED
ORNAMENTS

Fuzzy, festive, and fun. These felted orbs are made using a simple technique that can be played out in patterns as complex as your heart desires. Make a pile of these ornaments to give as holiday gifts, and you'll be lauded for your craft skills and design expertise. Nobody needs to know how easy it is to make these felted goodies.

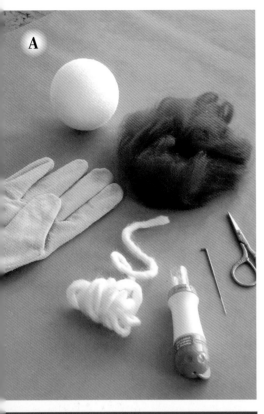

A

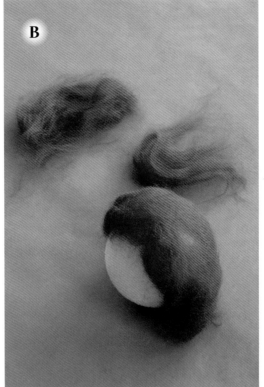

B

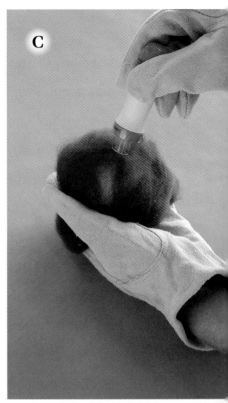

C

D

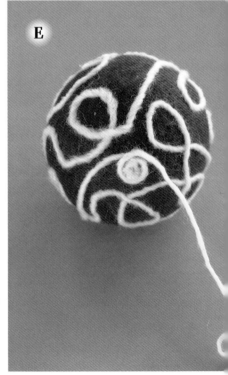

E

PREPARATION: Gather your tools, roving, and yarn. Don't forget the gloves! They should be made of leather that isn't too soft, so that a needle can't penetrate them. (photo A)

1 Gently tease a piece of wool off of the main clump of roving. Fan it out and lay it over a section of one of the styrofoam balls. (photo B)

2 Put the gloves on. Then grasp the wool roving tightly and hold it in place, making sure it covers the surface of the ball. Jab the roving gently with the needle-felting tool. Go over the surface of the ball thoroughly, making sure you keep your hand on the side of the ball that's opposite from the needle. As you finish working over one section with the tool, tear off and add new pieces of roving. Felt them into place with the tool until you've covered the entire ball. (photo C)

3 Add thin, wispy tufts of roving to any bald spots on the ball. Go over the entire surface again with the tool to thoroughly felt the wool. Work over any lumps a few extra times with the tool to tangle the threads deeper into the felted matrix.

NOTE ABOUT ADDING EMBELLISHMENTS: The number of variations on dots, squiggles, and geometric patterns that you can felt on the ornament might just be infinite.

The basic technique is demonstrated at left to create a random squiggle pattern, but you can use pieces of yarn or tiny clumps of wool roving to do all kinds of stuff. Use the ornaments shown in the picture as guides, and let your imagination fill in the blanks.

4 Lay a length of yarn on the felted surface of the ball, letting it loop, swirl, and zigzag as you like. With the gloves on, gently tack the yarn in place with a few punches of the felting tool. Once that yarn is secured in place, swirl the rest of the yarn length across the ornament to fill in the empty areas. Loops are always good, but so are U-turns, ands spirals. Be playful! You can always tear a section loose if you don't like how it looks. Tack the yarn in place with a few jabs of the felting tool as you go. (photo D)

5 Once you've covered the surface and are happy with the results, you'll want to make a hanging cord for the ornament. Spiral the yarn around the central point from which you want the ornament to hang. Circle the yarn around that point three or four times. With the tool (and with the gloves on), felt the spirals of yarn in place. Keep felting and adding more spirals (if needed) until you feel the hanging cord is securely attached. (photo E)

Christmas Beasts

FOR YOUR TREE

Now that you've learned the simple pleasures of felting wool onto styrofoam, try adding a little more character—and a whole lot more holiday adorableness—to the mix. These sweet little creatures might seem complicated to make, but you can easily populate your holiday tree with a whole wonderland of winter guests.

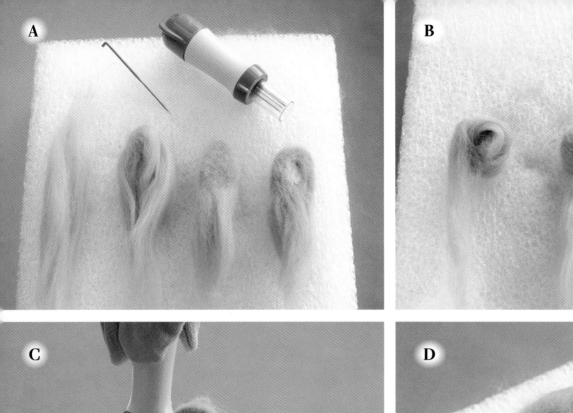

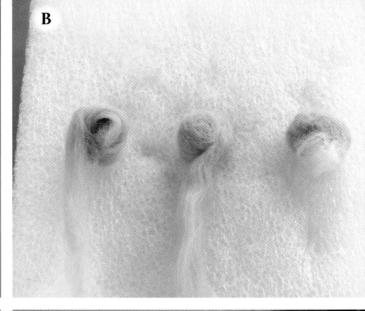

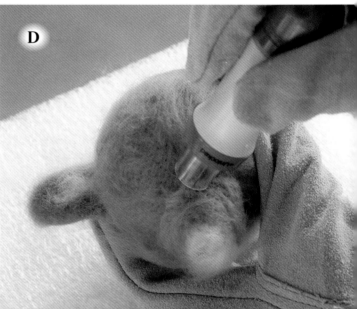

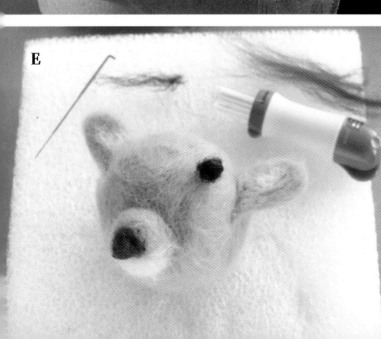

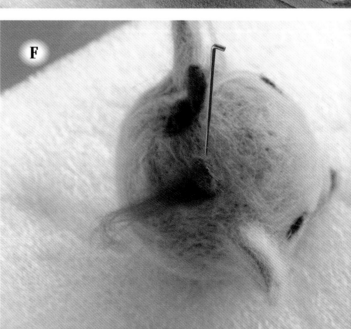

MATERIALS

styrofoam balls

wool roving in colors appropriate to the animals. For the reindeer:

beige, dark brown, black, white, red

yarn for hanging (optional)

TOOLS

needle-felting tool
(I like the punch that contains 4 needles)

and/or

regular single felting needle

heavy leather work gloves to protect your hands

foam felting mat (or thick piece of foam)

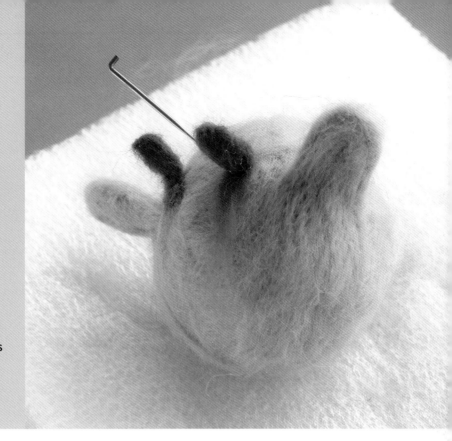

PREPARATION: To make the reindeer, start by covering one of the foam balls with the fawn- or beige-colored wool roving (see page 51 for instructions on how to do this). Remember to wear gloves throughout the felting process to protect your fingers from those sharp needles.

1 To make the ears: Take a haft of the beige roving that's about as thick as a finger and roughly 8 inches (20.3 cm) long, and fold it in half. Lay it on the foam pad and jab it repeatedly at the fold point with the needle-felting tool. The fibers will tangle together and form a firm shape. Aim your needle strokes so that they create the soft, rounded triangle of an ear. Once you're happy with the shape of the ear, add a small, pea-sized tuft of white wool to create the inner ear. Needle felt the white wool into place. Repeat this process for a second ear. (photo A)

2 The reindeer's snout is formed in a similar fashion. This time, start with a beige haft of roving. Roll one end of it into a spiraling ball and felt it with your tool. Roll and needle it until you're happy with the size—remember, it'll be serving as a snout. Add a tuft of white roving to one side of the ball for the reindeer's light-colored muzzle. (photo B)

3 To atttach the ears: A little tail of leftover roving should still be attached to each ear. Spread one of these tails across the ornament and jab it with the needle to secure it in place. Needle all around the base of the ear so that it's forced to stand up and is securely attached to the ornament. Then position the second ear on the other side of the felted sphere and needle it into place in the same fashion. (photo C)

4 To attach the snout: Based on the position of the ears, place the snout on the reindeer face so that the white muzzle is facing downward. Press the snout into place, and needle around its base to secure it. The edge of the snout will feather outward onto the felted sphere. If the seam between the snout and the sphere seems too prominent, cover it with a thin wisp of beige roving and needle into place. (photo D)

5 Roll a thin piece of red roving between your thumb and forefinger to make a pea-sized ball that will serve as the tip of the reindeer's nose. Roll a similarly sized pair of balls from black roving to serve as the reindeer's eyes. Needle these details into position. You may find that a single needle works better than a multi-needle tool for attaching these smaller details. (photo E)

6 Roll a short, fat noodle of dark-brown roving to make the antler buds. Felt the noodle on the foam mat until the buds are about an inch (2.5 cm) long and ¼ inch (6 mm) around, with a short tail of unfelted roving. Position the two buds between the ears on the top of the head, and felt each tail of roving into place. Then needle around the base of each antler so that it's forced to stand up and is secured in place. Cover any excess brown roving at the base of the antlers by needling a few wisps of beige wool into place. (photo F) Add a hanging loop as shown on page 51, if desired.

Soda Can
PUNCHED METAL TREES

Here's a beautiful, festive way to recycle aluminum soda cans. Carve delicate shapes from the silvery metal with a craft punch, and then use the pieces to embellish cardboard tree forms. These upcycled ornaments make great table toppers.

NOTE: Aluminum is a soft, easy-to-cut substance. However, your punches might not be made to cut metal. I've created dozens of these trees with my punches, and they continue to cut beautifully. Just keep in mind that this project may dull your punches over time. If you don't want to risk using them, you can easily make the trees from metallic paper.

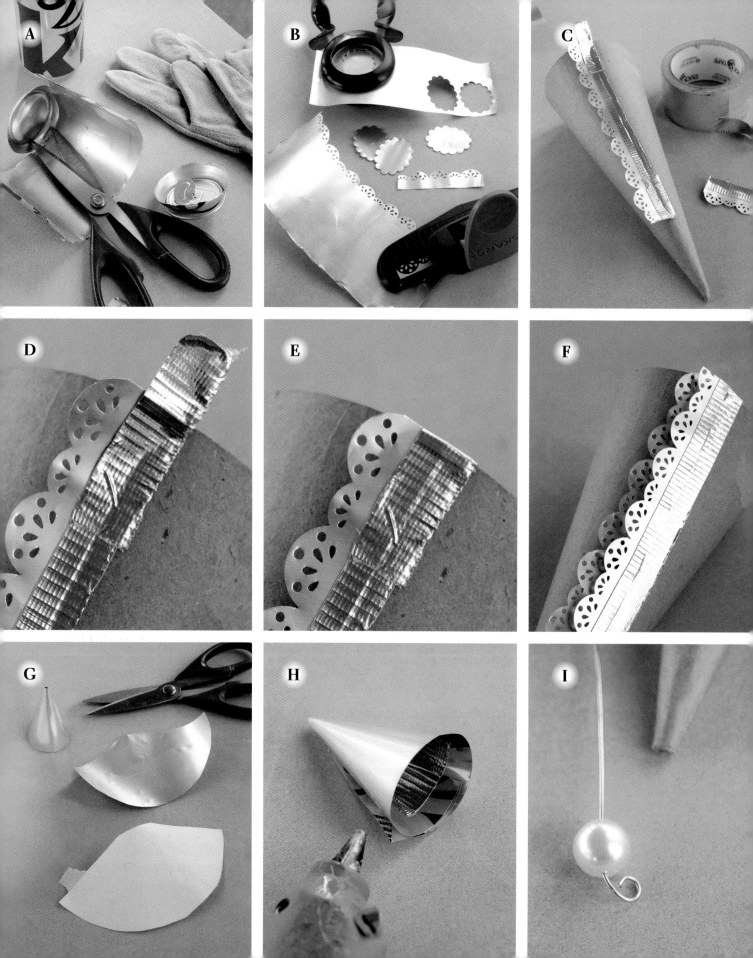

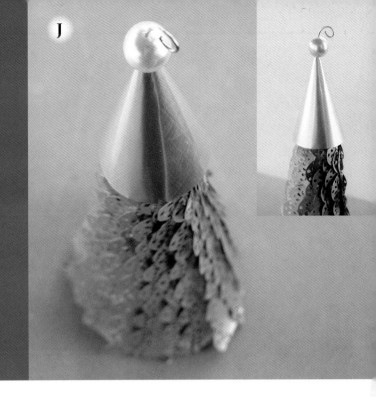

MATERIALS

6 to 12 soda cans, rinsed and dried

small chipboard tree form about 10 inches (25.4 cm) high

silver duct tape

short length of craft wire

small pearl bead or pearl topped straight pin, 3 inches (7.6 cm) long

TOOLS

heavy leather work gloves

craft scissors

border punch (for tree #1) or scalloped edge oval punch (for tree #2)

photocopier and printer

hot-glue gun

needle-nosed pliers

Tree #1

1 Wearing gloves and using the craft scissors, make a snip in the top edge of one of the soda cans where the side of the can meets the top. Snip around the top edge to remove the can top. Then cut straight down the side of the can and along the bottom edge to remove the bottom of the can. You should now have a clean sheet of flat aluminum. (photo A)

2 Use your border punch (following the manufacturer's instructions) to cut the first figured border out of the long side of the metal sheet. Then use the scissors to cut the figured edge off the aluminum sheet, leaving a strip of aluminum that's about ½ or ¾ inch (1.3 or 1.9 cm) wide below the punched edge. (photo B)

3 Tear or cut the silver duct tape to make a piece that's about ¾ inch (1.9 cm) wide and roughly 1 inch (2.5 cm) longer than the piece of punched border. Lay the tape down with the adhesive side up, and gently press the aluminum border onto it so the tape catches about ¼ inch (6 mm) of the metal. Position the taped border piece on the tree form so that the end of it is even with the bottom edge of the tree. The piece shouldn't extend all the way up to the tip of the tree, because the circumference at the tip is too small to accommodate the many layers of border bands needed to cover the tree. The pieces should stop 1 to 2 inches (2.5 to 5 cm) below the top of the tree. (photo C)

4 Let the short tail of extra tape hang over the bottom edge of the tree form as shown. (photo D)

5 Flip the overhanging tape over the bottom edge of the chipboard tree and secure it on the inside of the cone. (photo E)

6 Repeat step 3 with the next band of metal. Layer it over the first band, making sure that the pattern of the border is slightly offset so that more of the first band is revealed and the duct tape doesn't show between layers. Press the new band in place, and tuck in the over-hanging tape at the bottom as before. Keep adding new bands until the entire circumference of the tree is layered with them. (photo F)

7 To make the cone that fits over the top of the tree: Enlarge the template on page 128 to 200% and print it onto a piece of paper. Cut it out and bend it into a cone. Try it out on the tree to make sure it fits. It should cover the tip of the tree and extend down beyond the top edge of the layered metal bands. Adjust the sharpness of the cone until it fits comfortably on the tree. Then use the scissors to cut the template out of one of the pieces of aluminum sheet, and bend the metal into a cone as you did with the paper. (photo G)

8 Once you're happy with the fit of the cone, duct tape its interior to secure the shape. Then use the hot-glue gun to place a band of glue along the outside edge of the cone flap so that it will permanently hold its shape. (photo H)

9 Twist the end of the piece of craft wire into a small loop. Then thread the small pearl bead onto the wire, and push it up to the loop. Thread the other end of the wire down through the tiny hole in the top of the cone you created in step 7. Place a dot of hot glue on the end of the wire, and thread it into the top hole of the chipboard tree form. Press it all the way down so the cone fits snugly on the top of the tree and covers the raw edge of the layers of metal borders. (photo I and J)

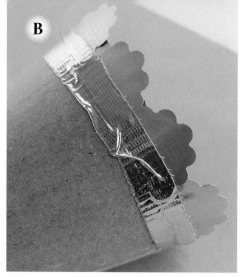

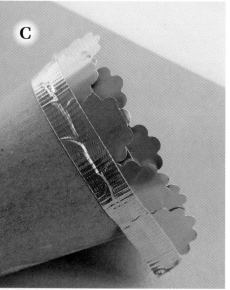

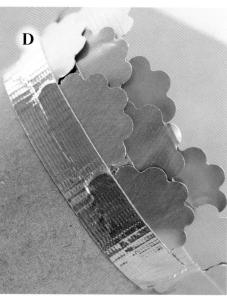

Tree # 2

1 This tree is made in a fashion similar to the first one. You'll use the same materials and tools, and the same cone template. However, this tree requires a different punch. It features scalloped-edge ovals cut out of soda-can metal. Once you've punched out the ovals, use the scissors to cut each of them in half the short way, as shown. (photo A)

2 Tear or cut a piece of silver duct tape about ½ x 8 inches (1.3 x 20.3 cm). Place the tape with the adhesive side up on your work surface, and press the cut ovals into it about ¼ inch (6 mm) down from the top edge of the tape. Place each oval snugly against its neighbor, but don't overlap the pieces. (photo A)

3 Wrap the tape with the metal pieces around the bottom edge of the chipboard tree form, aligning the bottom edge of the metal pieces with the bottom edge of the chipboard cone as shown. (photo B) Press the tape firmly to secure it in place. Add another piece of tape if needed to circle the entire circumference of the tree bottom.

4 Repeat step 2 to make more tape pieces with metal scallops. Then add another row of scallops and tape to the tree, making sure you overlap the tape from the previous row with the metal pieces on the new row. (This will ensure that the tape isn't visible.) Offset the oval pieces so that the valleys of the new row occur where the peaks from the preceding row appear. This makes for an attractive fish-scale effect that plays out delight-fully on the tree. (photo C)

5 Continue adding rows up the tree until you've covered it to within about 2 inches (5 cm) of the top. You may have to bend the metal scallops slightly as you near the top so that they wrap snugly around the tapering tree form. (photo D)

6 Follow steps 7 through 9 from tree #1 to finish the top cone of the tree. To secure the cone on this tree, I used a 3-inch (7.6 cm) pearlized pin instead of a bent wire with a pearl bead.

Lacy Stars
FOR HOLIDAY WINDOWS

Dress your windows in winter white this holiday season. Made from lace
and wire, these five-point stars will create lots of cheer—both inside
and outside your home—for many years to come.

MATERIALS

12-gauge aluminum craft wire (about as thick as an average coat hanger)

tape for marking the wire

clear packing tape to make the wire joint

lacy fabric (you'll need a piece large enough for covering the star with a few inches of overhang. A half yard— approximately 18 x 44 inches (45.7 x 111.8 cm)— should be enough to cover two 15-inch (38.1 cm) stars

white thread

white string or wire for hanging

TOOLS

tape measure

heavy leather work gloves to protect your hands

needle-nosed pliers/ wire cutters

sewing needle

fabric scissors

MEASURING YOUR WIRE: To make the star, you'll need a piece of wire that's approximately 10 times the length of each star point. In other words, if you want the star points to stick out about 5 inches (12.7 cm), you'll need about 50 inches (127 cm) of wire for the points. Always add about 6 extra inches (15.2 cm) to the length of your wire before you cut it to make sure you have enough to finish the star. You can easily cut off the extra wire in the last step. A star with 5-inch (12.7 cm) points will measure approximately 15 inches (38.1 cm) across.

PREPARATION: You'll need to work at a sturdy table or countertop that has a sharp 90° edge so that you can bend the wire. A small piece of wood or a cutting board will also come in handy.

1 If the 12-gauge wire came in a coil, straighten it as much as possible before you use it. Measure the approximate amount of wire needed (see note above), and cut it with the wire cutters. Run your gloved hands along the length of the wire using downward pressure with your thumbs to straighten out the wire as shown. (photo A)

2 Measure the wire and use tape to mark the points and the valleys of the star. Add an extra inch (2.5 cm) to the first segment of wire just to be safe, but mark the wire in even increments thereafter. For example, for a 15-inch ((38.1 cm) star, tape the first mark at 6 inches (15.2 cm), then measure nine more lengths of 5 inches (12.7 cm) each. You should have several inches of leftover wire.

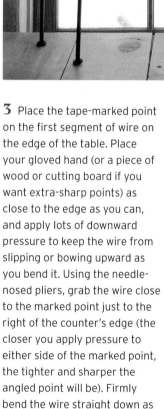

3 Place the tape-marked point on the first segment of wire on the edge of the table. Place your gloved hand (or a piece of wood or cutting board if you want extra-sharp points) as close to the edge as you can, and apply lots of downward pressure to keep the wire from slipping or bowing upward as you bend it. Using the needle-nosed pliers, grab the wire close to the marked point just to the right of the counter's edge (the closer you apply pressure to either side of the marked point, the tighter and sharper the angled point will be). Firmly bend the wire straight down as far as you can. (photos B and C)

4 To sharpen the angle of the bend, grasp the wire on either side of the point, placing your forefingers on the bend. Press firmly on the wire with the tips of your fingers to bend the wire sharply into a more acute point. (photo D)

5 Flip the wire over, and follow steps 3 and 4 to bend the next segment of wire in the opposite direction. This will produce an inward angle that will help define the star's points. (photo E) As you can see from the photo, what you're going for is a zigzagged wire, alternating back and forth, to make the star. (photo F) Continue bending the wire until you have five points and five valleys.

6 Roughly shape the star by keeping the points sharply angled and making the valley angles a little more oblique. Your first and last segments of wire should be cut to the correct length to form one spliced segment that provides the last side of one point of the star. Cut one segment to leave about 2 inches (5 cm) of wire. Cut the other segment to leave about 3 inches (7.6 cm). Once spliced, these two will make a 5-inch (12.7 cm) side. (photo G)

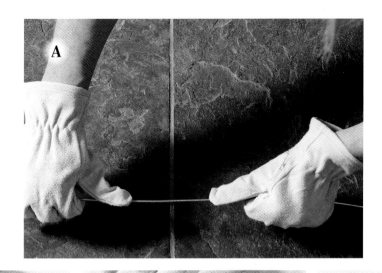

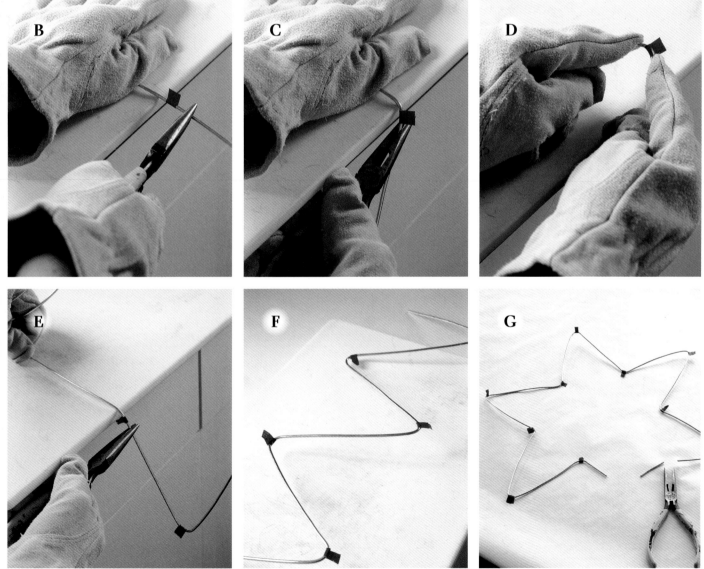

H

I

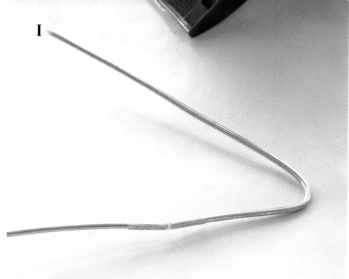

J

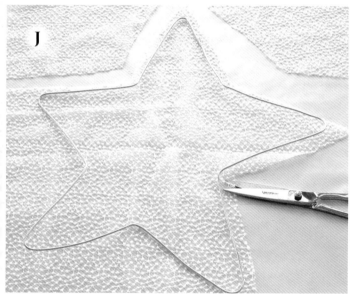

K

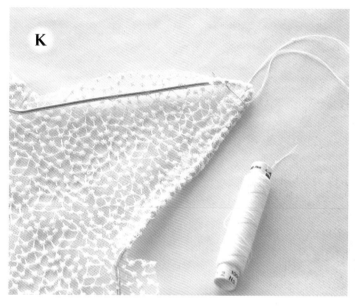

7 Bend and squeeze the star so that the angles leading up to the splice point on the last leg allow the ends to meet naturally, tip to tip, and not at an angle. Once you're happy with the shape of the star, place a short piece of clear packing tape on your work surface with the adhesive side up. Then position the two cut ends of the wire on the tape as close together as possible. Wrap the tape very tightly around this splice joint multiple times to make the joint as straight and even as possible. (photos H and I)

8 Place the wire star on the lace fabric and secure it with tape in a couple of places so that it can't move around. Cut the fabric around the star shape, leaving an extra inch (2.5 cm) or so of overhang. At each valley point in the star, make a straight cut in from the edge of the fabric to the wire, so that the fabric can wrap smoothly around each arm without bunching at the valley corners. Also, cut straight across the fabric at each point so that there isn't any excess fabric at the star's tips. (photo J)

9 Thread a needle with a double length of thread, and knot the end. Fold the excess fabric along the star's perimeter over the wire, and stitch the two layers of fabric together tightly using an overcast stitch. Your needle will go in through both layers of fabric, up and over the wire, around the back, and then up through the layers of fabric again, a little farther along than the first stitch. Continue stitching until you reach the first point. When you get there, fold down the fabric's snipped point, and then fold one side of the fabric over that and stitch it into place. Fold the fabric on the opposite side of the point in, and continue down the side using the overcast stitch. (photo K) Attach a length of string or wire to one of the star's points for hanging.

Wrapping Ideas

FROM THE CASBAH

Stop buying expensive, seen-it-all-before, pre-packaged packaging, and start delighting your friends with custom wrapping that puts a fresh spin on seasonal traditions. Inspired by the dizzying marketplaces of Morocco and the Grand Bazaar of Istanbul, these wraps are a colorful feast for the eyes. Take some inspiration from these photos, and embark on your own creative adventure.

Jewel-toned tissue paper adds lots of spark while keeping things inexpensive and environmentally friendly.

Metallic papers and foils bring richness and a sense of preciousness to packages, even when used sparingly.

Paper punches create gloriously filigreed, geometric ribbons and tiny decorative elements that will dance across your packages.

Patterned scrapbook paper can be judiciously cut to create eye-catching embellishments that are more beautiful than traditional ribbons and wraps.

Button & String
REPLACE RIBBON & BOW

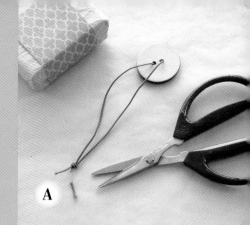

MATERIALS

elastic cord in various
colors and lengths

interesting/colorful
buttons and/or bells

TOOLS

scissors

A

TO MEASURE THE CORD:
Wrap it around your package
to measure the girth. Subtract
about an inch (2.5 cm) from
this length, then double the
length of cord.

1 Thread one length of cord
through the holes of a button
or the shank of a bell. Then
push the button or bell to the
center point of the cord, bring
the cord ends together to make
a large loop, and knot the ends.
Pull the knot tight, and trim the
cord ends close to the knot.
(photo A)

2 Wrap the cord around your
package, and slip the knotted
end of the loop over the button
to secure. **(photos B and C)**

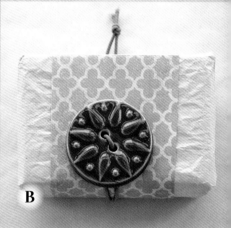

B

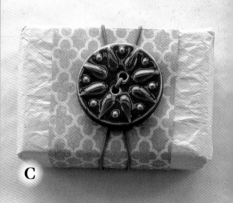

C

Bead Emboldened
ELIZABETHAN WREATH

Sophisticated, bejeweled, and beguiling—but edgy, too—
this wreath will add Elizabethan-era flair to your door or mantle.

MATERIALS

small foam wreath

cream-colored satin ribbon,
2 inches (5 cm) wide

PINS:
tiny, ½-inch (1.3 cm) stick pins

standard pearl-topped dressmaker pins

extra-long, 3-inch (7.6 cm) pearl-tipped pins

BEADS:
tiny metal beads in gold and silver

large, silver turban-shaped
corrugated beads

silver diamond-shaped beads

silver column beads

silver glass bugle beads

silver embroidery floss

TOOLS

scissors

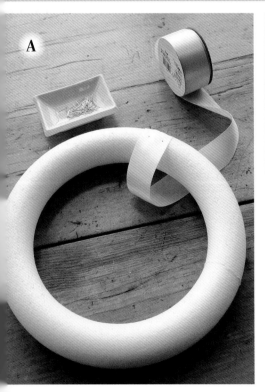

A

B

C

1 Secure the tail of the ribbon to the back of the foam wreath with two short pins. Then wrap the wreath in ribbon, securing the ribbon with one pin per wrap and making sure to slightly overlap the previous wrap each time. Finish by folding the ribbon end over about ½ inch (1.3 cm) and securing it with pins on the back. Then secure a large loop of ribbon with pins on the back of the wreath at the top to use as a hanger. (photo A)

2 Add beads to the front of the wreath at even intervals. For the first pass, alternate between a dressmaker's pin stuck through a plain gold bead and a dressmaker's pin stuck through a silver corrugated bead. To create even intervals between the beads, treat your wreath like a clock: Start with corrugated beads at 12, 3, 6, and 9 o'clock. Then center a plain gold bead between each of the corrugated beads. This should give you the reference points necessary to place the rest of the pins and beads at fairly even intervals. (photo B)

3 Add a row of dressmaker's pins with silver beads along the inside and outside of the wreath. Each bead should be positioned about halfway between the corrugated and plain beads placed in step 2. These pins will act as anchoring points for the zigzagging silver embroidery thread. (photo C)

4 Using the long, pearl-tipped pins, add the following: a column bead directly above the corrugated beads from step 2; a combination of a diamond-shaped bead, a small gold bead, and a bugle bead (used as a spacer) directly above the plain gold beads placed in step 2. Each of these fancy beads will be halfway between the plain beads added to the top row in step 3. This is easier than it sounds! Use the pictures below for guidance. (photo D)

5 Tie one end of the silver embroidery floss around a pin that holds a large corrugated bead, and tuck the tail of floss beneath the bead so it doesn't show. Then zigzag the floss down to the lower course of beads and back up to the middle course. Go up and down between courses until you've gone all the way around the wreath. (photo E) Once you return to the starting bead, repeat the same zigzagging path, but alternate between the middle and the upper courses of beads. Once you return to the starting bead, tie the floss end securely to the pin, and tuck any remaining floss beneath the bead. (photo F)

Folk Art
FELTED COASTERS

Some of the most evocative holiday designs are often the simplest. These felted coasters feature a classic geometric pattern that's easy to create and graphically striking. Perfect for your holiday libations! If you've never felted before, this quick project is the perfect place to start.

1 Using the CD as a template, trace circles onto the colored felt and cut them out with the scissors. Then stack three different-colored circles on top of each other, and pin them together. Machine-sew around the perimeter of the stacked circles about ¼-inch (6 mm) in from the edge. You can trim the circles closer to the stitching to neaten up the edges, if you like. (photo A)

2 Place the felted coaster on the foam mat. Tease off a piece of wool roving that's about as thick as your finger and 6 inches (15.2 cm) long. Grab it in the middle and give it a couple of firm twists. Place the center of the twist in the center of the coaster. Put your gloves on, and then jab the needle-felting tool repeatedly into the center of the wool tuft so that the roving fibers get tangled into the felted wool fabric. This is felting! (photo B)

3 Grab a tuft of roving by the end and gently pull on it as you needle felt along its length. Jab it repeatedly with the needle(s) so that the roving gets incorporated into the fabric. Continue pulling gently as you needle the wool. This will make a slim, nicely pointed shape. (photo C)

4 Once the roving is felted into the fabric, grab the very tip of the wisp of wool and pull it fairly hard—even twirl it—as you needle the wool. You're actually pulling out a bit of the wool to leave the sharpest, smallest point. Keep pulling and needling all the way out to the end. (photos D and E) Repeat on the opposite point.

5 Repeat steps 2 through 4 to add additional tufts to make a 6- or 8-point star on your coaster. To add the dots between the points, roll a pea-sized piece of roving between your thumb and forefinger, position it on the coaster as shown, and felt it with your tool until it flattens into the coaster. (photo F)

MATERIALS

¼ yard (.25 m) 100% wool or wool-blend felt in each of the following colors: cream, gray, red, and olive green

natural-white wool roving

white thread

TOOLS

CD (as template)

pen or pencil for tracing template

scissors

straight pins

sewing machine

needle-felting tool (I like the punch that contains 4 needles) and/or regular single felting needle

foam felting mat

heavy leather work gloves

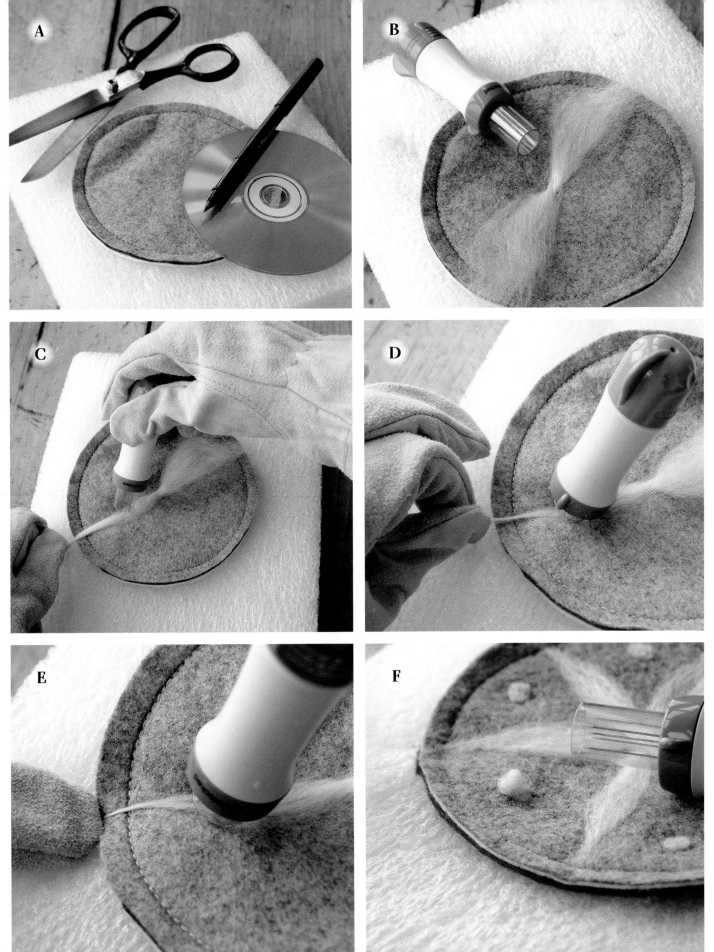

Wool-on-Linen
TABLE RUNNER

A length of linen and a bit of wool are all you need to make this elegant yet earthy table runner. The charming design—part star, part poinsettia—is needle-felted. Holiday elegance doesn't get any easier than this!

MATERIALS

½ yard (.5 m) natural linen fabric, 54-60 inches (137.2 to 152.4 cm) wide

natural-white wool roving

a bit of gold- or camel-colored roving

white or cream thread

TOOLS

scissors

needle-felting tool (I like the punch that contains 4 needles) and/or regular single felting needle

foam felting mat

heavy leather work gloves

sewing machine

PREPARATION: Cut the length of linen to the desired size for your finished table runner. I've found that 15 inches (38.1 cm) is a good width for most tables. The runner can overhang your table ends by a foot (30.5 cm) or so or stop short of the edges by 6 to 12 inches (15.2 to 30.5 cm)—it's up to you. (A longer, overhanging runner may need a seam down the middle to make the fabric long enough.) Once you've felted the runner, iron the back of it with a steam iron to fluff the designs so that they're even more prominent against the background fabric.

1 The technique for this project is similar to that used in the Folk Art Coasters project on page 74. The star/poinsettia shapes on the runner vary in size. You can select the size and placement of the various felted patterns as you work the piece. The photos above and at right (A through D), show the process fairly succinctly. Refer to the Folk Art Coasters project on page 77 for more in-depth instructions on how to felt the starry shapes. **(photos A through D)**

2 Felt little dots on the ends of the starry points. Add little dots of camel-colored roving to the center of each star for a spot of color. Keep adding starry shapes to your runner until you're happy with it. **(photo D)**

3 To finish the edge of your runner, use your sewing machine to topstitch around the outside perimeter about ¾ inch (1.9 cm) from the edge. You can fray the outside edge by using a pin to pick up a piece of the linen thread within the weave of the fabric along the edge and gently pulling it all the way up the side of the fabric until it comes out. Remove thread from each side of the runner in this fashion until you're satisfied with the amount of fraying you've created. **(photo E)**

B

C

D

E

Folded Page SNOWFLAKES

This simple, meditative project is perfect for bookworms who have a stash of discarded paperbacks lying around. You can make a flurry of these bookish snowflakes in no time. A sprinkle of glass glitter adds just the right amount of sparkle to each ornament, so they can spin in a holiday window and catch the rays of winter sun.

MATERIALS

paperback book

double-stick tape

spray adhesive

silver or gold glass glitter

string for hanging

TOOLS

craft knife and
cutting surface

straightedged ruler

knife or spoon for
sprinkling glitter

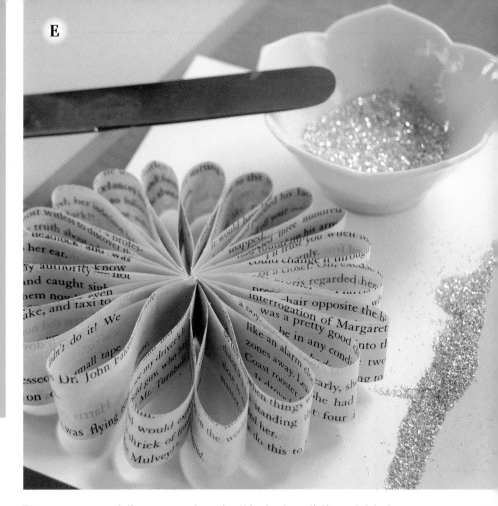

PREPARATION: Remove the cover from the paperback so that the book pages and glued spine are revealed. Tear or cut the spine vertically to create a glued cluster or pad of about 30 pages.

1 With the craft knife and a ruler, cut a strip of the book pad that's about 1-inch (2.5 cm) wide. (photo A)

2 Place a small strip of double-stick tape on the first page of the book strip, and bend the first page around so that it sticks to the tape and forms a petal shape. Push this petal forward (as though you're turning a page of the book) and repeat the taping and bending step with the next page to create a second petal shape. (photo B)

3 Continue taping and bending until you have enough petals to make a nice full circle as shown. Tear away extra pages if you have more than you need, but leave a small cluster at the end that's straight and unbent to use for hanging. (photo C)

4 Spray the ornament with adhesive. Using the spoon or knife, sprinkle the glitter over the wet adhesive and shake off the excess. Place a folded piece of paper beneath the snowflake as you sprinkle for easy cleanup. (photos D and E)

There are many variations you can try using this simple, radiating petal design. Try folding every other page in half with a sharp fold. Or fold every other page in half with a sharp fold and then press the tip of the fold inward to make a Y-shaped page (see below). You can also alternate between the sharp fold and the Y fold.

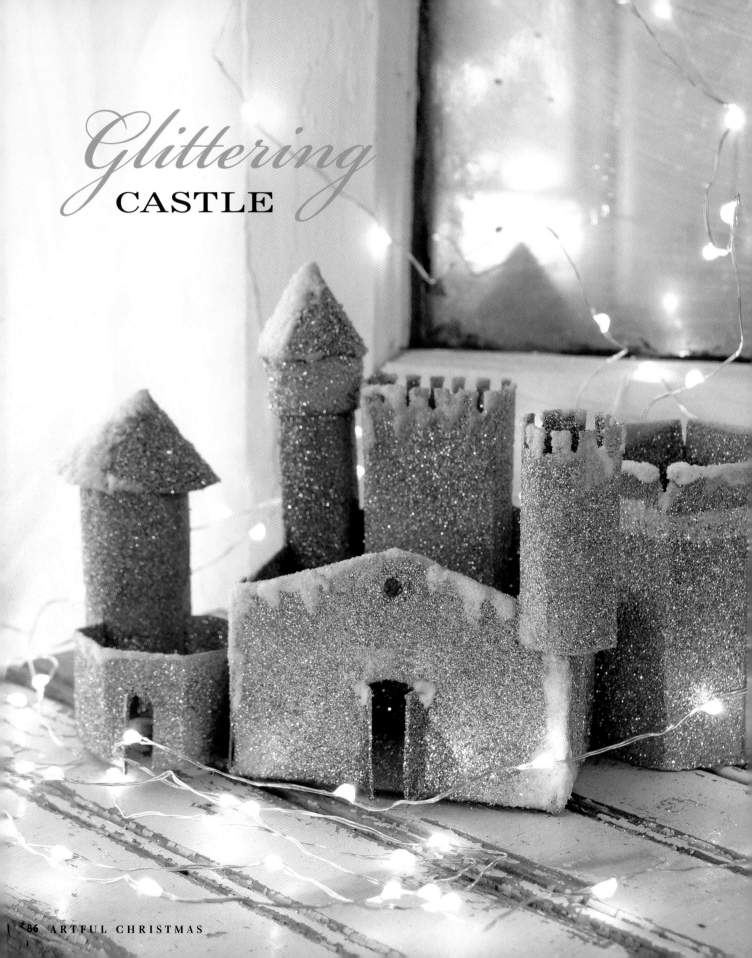

Glittering CASTLE

This year, all I want for Christmas is a small castle glistening in a snowy field. Does that seem like too much to ask? Not when you can make a sparkling jewel like this one with your very own hands. This project might look involved, but none of the steps are difficult. The process is more fun than putting together a puzzle, and the result is unique and precious.

MATERIALS

template, page 126

poster board

repositionable gluestick

white glue

spray or craft paint for castle background color (optional)

spray adhesive or glitter glue

glass glitter in various colors, including white and silver

TOOLS

copier or scanner/printer

scissors

craft knife

paper hole punch

bone folder or knife

clothespins

dowels, fat pencils, wooden spoons, or knitting needles for rolling poster board

small paintbrush

knife or spoon for sprinkling glitter

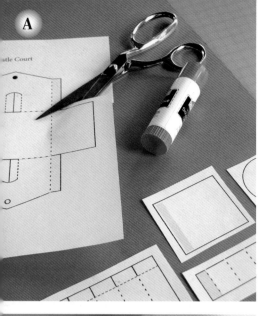

A

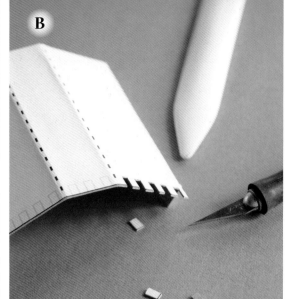

B

C

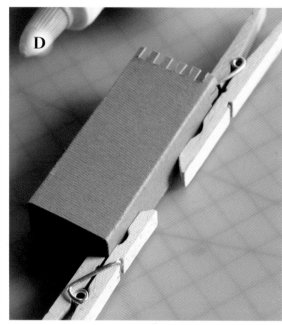

D

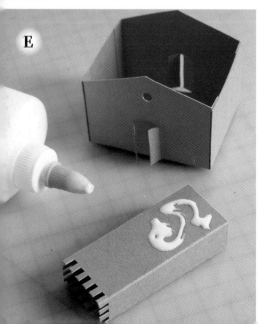

E

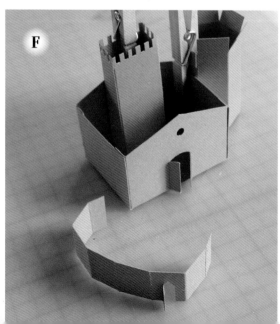

F

PREPARATION: Copy and enlarge the castle template pieces on page 126. Note that the solid lines are cutting lines, and the dotted lines are for folding. The gray areas are tabs for gluing.

1 Apply the repositionable glue to the back of each template, and stick them to the poster board. Use the sharp scissors and/or craft knife to cut out the pieces. (photo A) Use the hole punch to create the round window at the top of the main castle courtyard piece.

2 With the bone folder or the back of the knife, score the dotted lines before folding. A craft knife works great for smaller, more intricate cuts like the crenellated turrets and doors. Cut and fold all of the castle pieces as per the templates. (photo B)

3 Apply white glue to the tabs to adhere the pieces, and clamp the glue joints with clothespins while they dry. (photos C and D) Glue and clamp all of the pieces of the castle as directed by the templates.

4 Glue the square crenellated rampart to the inside of the back wall of the castle courtyard. Clamp it in place. (photo E) Glue and clamp the hexagonal tower onto the right side wall of the courtyard toward the back. Fold the fence for the castle yard on the dotted lines, and glue the tabs to the left side of the castle courtyard. (photo F)

5 Getting the poster board to roll into a tight tower shape without creases and folds can be hard. Try rolling the poster board around a series of increasingly smaller objects—the dowels, fat pencils, wooden spoon handles, and knitting needles. Once the poster board rolls gracefully, form it into a tower shape, and then glue and clamp it. Roll, glue, and clamp all of the tower pieces. Remember to add the extra piece of poster board on the base of the smallest tower to make it a little thicker at the top. Let everything dry. (photo G)

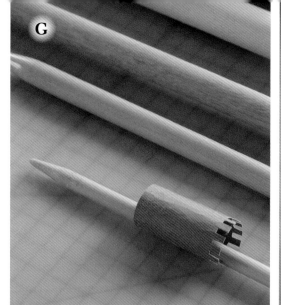

6 Roll the tower roofs around one of the dowels to soften the paper so that they form nice cones. Before you glue the cone flaps together to make each roof, try them on the tower bases. Then roll them to the proper size, glue, and clamp them. Let them dry. (photo H)

7 Put a generous stripe of white glue around the top edge of the tower base. Add a generous amount of white glue to the inside of the roof cone, and place the roof on the base. There's no good way to clamp this glue joint, so just hold the roof steady for a minute or two so the glue can set, and then leave it to dry undisturbed. (photo I)

8 Once the tower is dry, cut two slits directly opposite each other in the sides of the base (at 12 and 6 o'clock). The cut should go up the side about $3/8$ inch (1 cm). Do this on all of the tower bases. (photo J)

9 Slide the small crenellated tower onto the front right corner of the castle courtyard with one slit on the front wall and one on the right side wall. Slide the small turret tower on the left back corner of the courtyard. Place the large tower toward the back of the yard wall. (photo K)

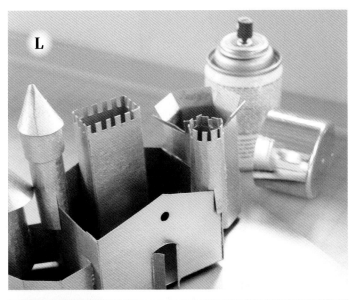

L

M

N

O

10 Feel free to leave the poster board its original color and add glitter to it. I covered one castle with metallic paint and another with blue paint before adding the glitter. Spray paint is the easiest way to apply color, but you can use craft paint and a brush as well. Let the paint dry thoroughly. (photo L)

11 Spray or brush on a layer of the adhesive. Make sure you cover the entire visible surface with the adhesive so that the glitter will stick to all of the parts. (photo M)

12 Sprinkle the glitter over the castle using the spoon or the tip of the knife. Put a piece of paper down before you add the glitter. You can pick up the paper when you're done and funnel the glitter back into its original container. I used gold glitter with a dusting of silver for the body of the castle. (photo N)

13 Add interest and authenticity to your castle by applying adhesive to certain details and sprinkling on glitter in a contrasting color. I chose copper-colored glitter for the roofs, green for the turrets, and red for the doors and windows. (photo O)

14 To add snow to your castle, dab glue liberally on the areas where flakes would logically settle—on roofs, atop walls, in nooks and crannies—and sprinkle white glass glitter over the glue. Add a light dusting of silver to make the snow really sparkle.

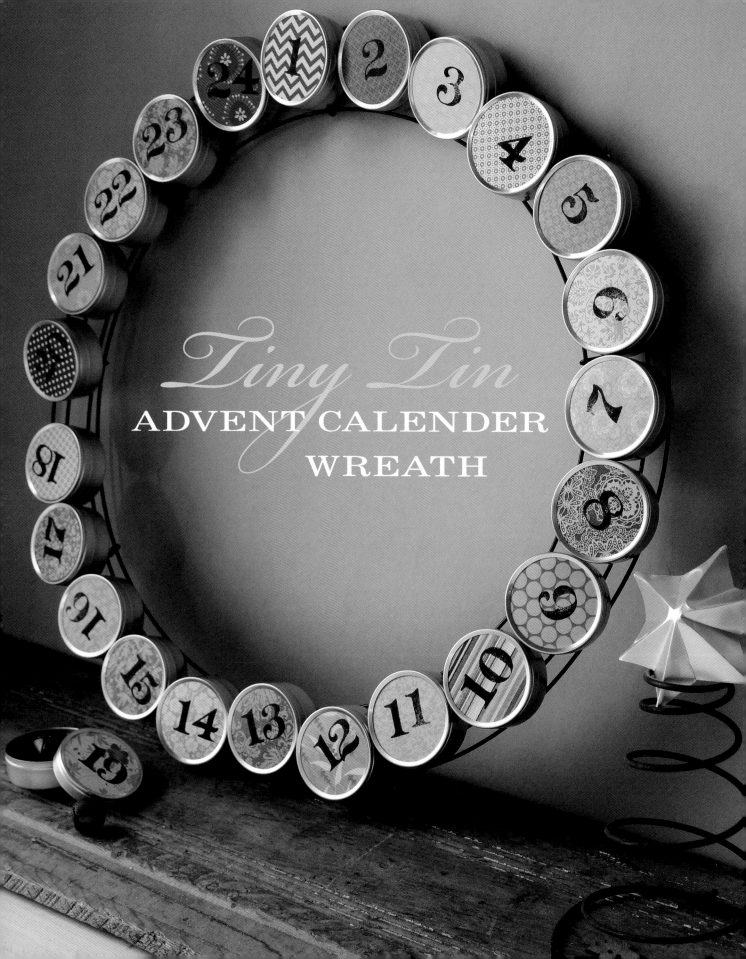

Tiny Tin
ADVENT CALENDER
WREATH

And the countdown begins!

Christmas is too exciting to be contained within a single day. Celebrate this expansive season with an advent calender to remind you that each day is a precious treat. Featuring holiday hues, this simple, graphic wreath lets you decorate with style and substance.

MATERIALS

variety of patterned paper

24 small, round metal tins

stamp pad

glue that adheres to metal

24 round magnets

metal wreath base

TOOLS

circle-cutting tool or paper punch

number stamps
(1 through 24)

A

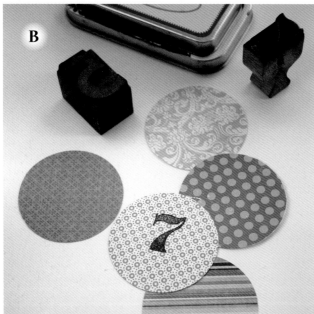

B

C

1 Use a circle-cutting tool or trace the lid of one the boxes onto paper to make circles for the tops of the tins. You'll need 24 circles cut from a variety of colored and patterned papers. (photo A)

2 Stamp each circle with a number from 1 through 24. Let the circles dry. (photo B)

3 Tuck a circle into the lid of one of the tins behind the transparent plastic front. The circle should fit snugly in place. If you want the tin to have less gloss and glare, remove the plastic lens, tuck the circle into the lid first (number-side out, of course), and then snap the plastic piece in behind it. The plastic will add rigidity to the paper.

4 Apply a dollop of the metal-friendly glue to the back of one of the magnets. Center the magnet on the back of the tin, and press it into place. Hold the magnet in place for a minute while the glue begins to set. Let the tin dry. (photo C)

5 Stash a fun little treat in the tin—something small and precious and sweet (edible or not). Nothing too heavy.

6 Repeat steps 3 through 5 to assemble the remaining 23 tins. Then stick them on the metal wreath frame—the magnets will hold them in place. You can line the tins up in ascending order or make the nightly hunt for advent treasure more challenging by mixing them up a bit. The wreath can be hung or propped casually against a wall or mantle.

Cookie Cutter
GARLAND

The soft metallic glow of this festive garland will brighten any corner.

A clever ribbon-and-bead attachment allows you to easily adjust its length.

Look for inexpensive vintage cookie cutters in junk stores or online.

Their nostalgic shapes will add sweet spice to your holiday hearth.

A

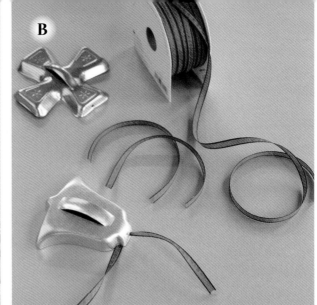

B

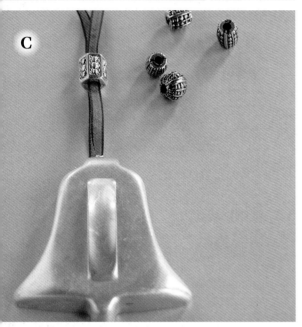

C

D

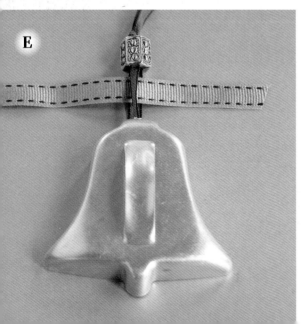

E

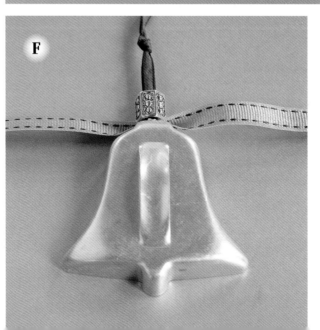

F

MATERIALS

vintage metal cookie cutters (a dozen or so)

2 to 3 yards (1.8 to 2.7 m) ribbon, ¼ inch (6 mm) wide, for attachments

2 to 3 yards (1.8 to 2.7 m) ribbon, ½ inch (1.3 cm) wide, for the length of the garland

large metal beads (one per cookie cutter)

TOOLS

small hammer

small nail

scrap of board

scissors

1 Use the hammer, nail, and scrap of wood to make a hole in the top of one of the cookie cutters. The hole doesn't need to be large—a few taps with the hammer and nail into the sidewall of the cutter should do the trick. (photo A)

2 Cut about 6 inches (15.2 cm) of the ¼-inch (6 mm) ribbon and thread it through the hole in the cookie cutter. (photo B)

3 Even up the ends of the ribbon as shown and slide a bead down both strands. Tie the two ribbons together in a knot above the bead so it can't slip off. Repeat steps 1 through 3 with the other cookie cutters. (photos C and D)

4 To make the garland, cut a length of the ½-inch (1.3 cm) ribbon and thread it through the loop below the bead in one of the narrow ribbon attachments. Secure the cookie cutter on the garland by pulling the bead down until it cinches snuggly against the top of the cutter. String the other cookie cutters onto the garland in the same way. Adjust their positions until you're pleased with the array, and cinch them into place. (photos E and F)

Snipped Paper CARDS

Spread the cheer this year with seasonal salutations you make yourself. Sure to warm up the coldest winter day, these high-spirited holiday greetings are loaded with fun colors and festive patterns.

MATERIALS

patterned paper

cardstock for the card
blank (printed or plain,
but with a light color
on the back for writing)

envelopes

glue

TOOLS

scissors

hole punch

heavy book
(for use as weight)

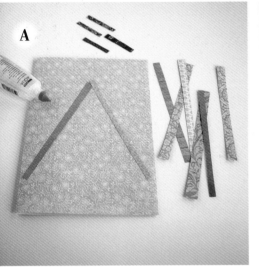

A

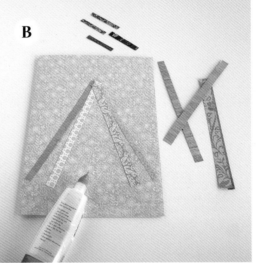

B

C

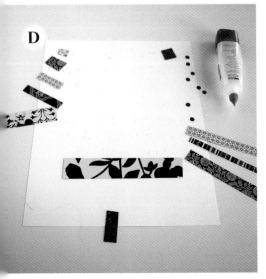

D

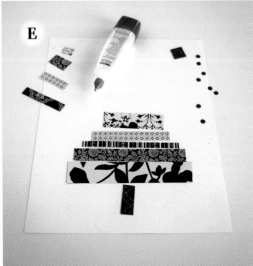

E

F

PREPARATION: You can find wonderful books of patterned paper in the scrapbooking section of your favorite craft store. You'll need heavyweight paper or cardstock and a selection of paper with subtle patterns for the card backgrounds. For the snips and dots that comprise the trees, select a variety of punchy patterns and colors you can mix up. Cut the patterned paper into narrow strips, and use the hole punch to create dots of different colors.

1 Fold a piece of the heavy paper or cardstock in half to make a nice-sized card that will fit in your envelope. For the vertical strip tree: Cut all of the paper strips to the same length to fit the height of your card. Spread a little glue on two of the strips and use them to create the outer edges of the tree as shown. **(photo A)**

2 Add the interior strips to fill out the tree. **(photo B)** Add a series of shorter, narrower, crisscrossing strips to make a star at the top of the tree as

shown. **(photo C)** Place the book on top of the card to make sure it dries flat.

3 For the horizontal strip tree: Cut 8 or 9 strips of patterned paper in slightly varying widths. Cut each one $\frac{1}{2}$ to 1 inch (1.3 to 2.5 cm) shorter in length as you move up the tree. Apply glue to the strips, and then build the tree from the bottom up, one strip at a time. Add a short vertical piece at the bottom for the tree's base. **(photos D and E)**

4 Add a bright little square or circle in a contrasting color to the top of the tree as a star. Put a dot of glue on the small punched circles, and sprinkle them around the tree as ornaments. Press them firmly into place. Place the book on top of the card to make sure it dries flat. **(photo F)**

MUSLIN BAG
Advent Calender

Pretty embellished bundles dangle from a cluster of twigs for an unexpected take on the traditional advent calendar. The drawstring pouches are unbleached muslin party-favor bags from the craft store. Simple-to-do embellishments with rubber stamps and fabric pens lend the bags vintage French feed-sack chic and hint that something wonderful is tucked inside.

PREPARATION: Use the paper punches to cut stencil pieces out of the poster board that you'll use for masking off the rubber stamp-impressions on the bags. Save both the punched-out shapes AND the poster board pieces they were cut out of. Using the knife or craft scissors, cut a narrow piece of poster board to use as a mask and a couple of plain poster board circles. You should also cut a piece of poster board that will fit into the muslin bag to make it firm while you apply the stamps and stencils. The cardboard will also keep the ink from bleeding through to the other side of the bag.

MATERIALS

small pieces of chipboard or poster board

24 small muslin favor bags

TOOLS

paper punches in scalloped square and scalloped oval

craft knife or scissors

circle cutter (optional)

large rubber stamps in allover patterns of graphic leaves, filigrees, or swashes (a multi-patterned block works great!)

ink pads in red and black

fine-tip permanent ink or fabric pens

small stencil numbers

small foam pounces

rubber stamp numbers

A

B

C

D

1 Use a masking piece like this scalloped square to contain the leafy motif of your rubber stamp. Position it on the muslin bag (either straight or on the diagonal). Then ink the rubber stamp and stamp it within the masked area. (photo A)

2 Trace the mask with the fine-tipped pen to outline a scalloped edge around the stamped background. (photo B)

3 Place one of number stencils in the center of your stamped design. Ink one of the small foam pounces and jab it into the stencil until you're happy with the density of the color. (photo C)

4 Add simple decorative elements like the dots shown here to make your design more detailed and interesting. (photo D)

GET CREATIVE AND PLAY: Check out the examples of decorative designs on the bags pictured on pages 102 and 103. Feel free to copy those techniques, but try inventing a few of your own! Two more alternatives are shown at right. Here's how they were done:

TOP RIGHT: Mask out the middle section of the bag with a strip of poster board. Then create the leafy background square with one of the stamps. Use the fine-tip pen to outline the blank center, adding a bracket detail on either end topped with a little dot. Use rubber-stamped numbers in the central blank. With the pen, add a line of detail inside the numbers for a little refinement.

BOTTOM RIGHT: Ink one of the large pounces and make a lightly colored circle in the center of one of the bags. Use a mask cut with a slightly larger circle to print a leafy pattern in a contrasting color over the pounced circle. Add a rubber-stamped number to the center.

Sand Painted
ORNAMENTS

I love adding glitter to simple objects, but not everything in life needs to sparkle. These wooden ornaments are coated in colored sand, which gives them an organic, suede-like texture. Metallic paint adds surface detail to create an ornament with undeniable rustic charm.

MATERIALS

wooden snowflake
blanks from the
craft store

a short length of
craft wire or a
few paper clips

spray adhesive or
white glue

colored craft sand

metallic dimensional
paint in fine-tipped
dispensers

spray finish
(optional)

string or cord
for hanging

TOOLS

drill with small bit

paintbrush for glue

small container
for pouring sand
over the ornament

1 Use the drill and the small bit to make a hole in the top of one of the ornaments. Thread the piece of wire or an unbent paper clip through the hole so that you have something to hold on to during the sanding process. Later, you can use the same hole for hanging the ornament. (photo A)

2 Spray the ornament with the adhesive or paint it with the white glue so that the sand will adhere to the wood. (photo B)

3 Working over a folded piece of paper (so that you can funnel the leftover sand back into its container), pour the sand over the ornament. To make sure the ornament is completely covered, you can lay it in the sand. Let it dry completely for a few hours or overnight. (photo C)

4 Add the dimensional paint elements: Make stripes down the center of the rays of the snowflake using metallic white. (photo D) Add dots on either side of the stripes in the same color. (photo E)

5 Add short strokes of gold metallic paint so that they radiate off of the white stripes, as shown. (photo F) Put a large dot of gold paint in the center of the snowflake. Finish off the ornament with a series of large, copper-colored dots that radiate around the center. (photo G)

6 Apply a coat of spray finish, if desired. When the ornament is dry, hang it on the tree with a cord or string.

F

E

G

Silvered Glass
VOTIVE HOLDERS

Pair easy-to-find mirrored glass spray paint with lacy
stencils to make elegant patterned votive holders.
The paint gives the holders a lit-from-within glow.

MATERIALS

assorted plain glassware:
votive holders, small
glasses, or clean jars

mirror-like spray paint
(available at craft and
hardware stores)

small pieces of lace in
various patterns

masking tape

spray paint in metallic
gold and gloss white

TOOLS

small plastic
shopping bag

scissors

1 Spray the inside of one of your votive holders with the mirror-like spray paint. To prevent the paint from getting on the outside of the glass (and to keep your hands paint free), put your hand inside the plastic shopping bag and then grasp the glass. Move your hand and the bag up to the rim of the glass and hold it tightly so that only the interior of the glass is showing. (photo A)

2 Spray the inside of the glass with the paint, making several light passes so that the paint doesn't drip. Follow the manufacturer's instructions to get an even coat of coverage. Let the glass dry. (photo B)

3 Cut a piece of lace that's big enough to wrap around the votive glass so that its two ends meet. Lay a strip of masking tape down with the adhesive side up. Then lay the edge of the lace on the tape so that it's secured. Make sure enough tape remains free below the edge of the lace so that it can be adhered to the glass. (photo C)

4 Tape the lace to the glass, adding a small piece of masking tape at the seam to hold the ends of the lace together. Try not to use too much tape at the seam—it can mask the paint and interfere with the lacy design on the glass. (photo D)

5 Spray the surface of the glass with the metallic gold or white paint. Use repeated light, even strokes to avoid drips. This coat doesn't need to be heavy—you just want a whisper of lace on the surface. (photo E)

6 Carefully remove the tape and the lace. Let the votive holder dry completely before using. (photo F)

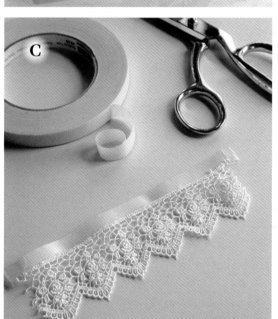

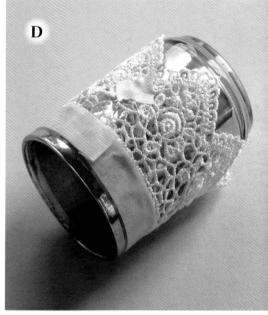

COLOR-BLOCKED
Gift Bags

This sculptural felt bag will add a bit of sophistication to any bottle of spirits. Stitching it is a breeze—you can make a half-dozen in an hour! Choose between jovial pom-poms and a more refined button-and-string closure for the perfect finishing touch.

MATERIALS

¼ yard (.25 cm) of felt (100% wool or a wool blend) in various colors, like cream, charcoal gray, red, and olive green

thread in contrasting colors

for the pom-pom closure:

yarn

elastic hair band (optional)

for the button-and-string closure:

colored elastic cord

button

TOOLS

straightedged ruler

scissors

stick pins

sewing machine

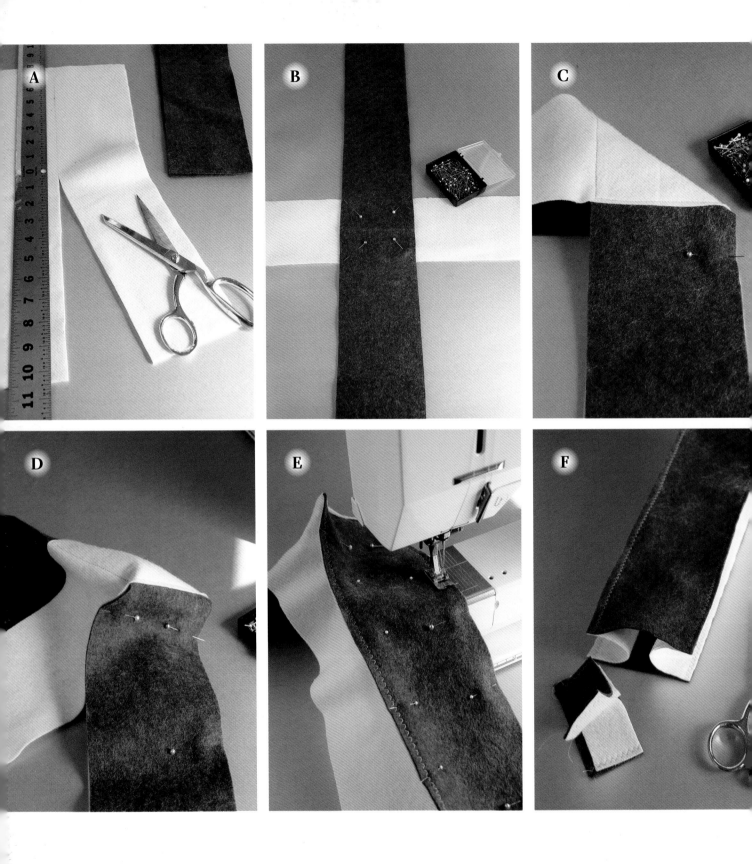

MAKING THE GIFT BAG: Sew the bottle bag in interesting, contrasting colors of felt, then add more contrast with brightly colored, zigzagging thread. The fuzzy pom-poms add another pop of color (see directions below), or go with the natty button-and-string bow on page 114 for a more sophisticated (and quicker!) closure.

1 Mark and cut a strip of felt that's about 4 x 36 inches (10.2 x 91.4 cm). Cut a strip of the same size from a contrasting color of felt. (photo A)

2 Position the two felt pieces so that they're perpendicular to one another and cross at their center points. Pin the pieces and then sew them together by stitching a square about 1/8 inch (3 mm) in from the edge of the fabric, all the way around the point of overlap. This will form the base of the bottle bag. (photo B)

3 Fold the newly sewn base on the diagonal, and bring the side pieces of felt up to meet each other. In the photo at left, the cream-colored side piece of felt meets up with the gray side

piece. Pin the two pieces together all the way up the side. (photo C)

4 Fold up the other cream-colored side piece so that it meets the other gray side piece to make the second seam and define the front of the bag. Pin the pieces to secure. (photo D)

5 Using a zigzag stitch and contrasting thread, sew up the two pinned sides of the bag. Flip the bag over, and repeat steps 3 through 5 to complete the back of the bag. (photo E) Cut the bag straight across the top to even up the edges. You can adjust the height of the bag to accommodate the size of your bottles. (photo F)

POM-POM TIE: Why buy elaborate tools for whipping up pom-poms when your fingers can do the job just fine?

1 Wrap the yarn around your fingers (two fingers for a small pom-pom; three for a larger one). The more times you wrap the yarn, the fatter the pom-pom will be. (photo A)

2 Slide the yarn off your fingers, and use a bit of it

to tie the mass tightly in the middle. (photo B)

3 Slide your scissors through the loops of yarn above the knot and cut through them. Do the same with the loops below the center knot. (photo C)

4 Give your pom-pom a haircut, snipping off errant yarn to form a nice round ball. (photo D)

5 Tie the two tails of yarn from the knot in the center of the pom-pom to an elastic hair band. Knot the tails tightly, and then snip the leftover yarn.

Add two more pom-poms to make an ample cluster for your bottle bag.

Or you can tie the pom-poms to a twisted or braided bit of yarn and use it as a ribbon tie for the bag. (photo E)

DOUBLE
Circle Wreath

This vibrant wreath provides an eye-catching pop of holiday cheer. Its bright, rich colors will help you banish the winter blues and welcome the holidays with a smile.

A

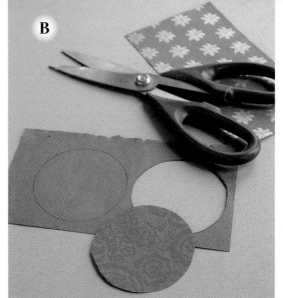

B

C

D

E

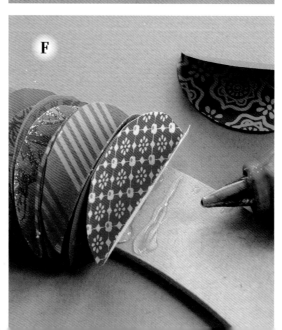

F

PREPARATION: Collect patterned paper in rich shades of red, orange, and magenta. Add a few sheets in varying shades of green to create a lively mix.

1 Decide on a size for your circles. You want to make efficient use of your paper, so go with a size that's not too big. I made my wreath from circles with a diameter of about 2 ½ inches (6.4 cm). (photo A)

2 Use a circle cutter to make the circles. If you don't have one, try stacking a few sheets of paper on top of each other and tracing a circle on the top sheet using a glass or lid for a template. Then cut the circles out of the stack of paper with the scissors. You'll be surprised at how quickly the cutting goes. (photo B)

3 Fold the circles in half in the center. The side that you want to be visible in the wreath should be folded toward the inside. (photo C)

4 Use the glue gun to apply a stripe of adhesive to the wooden wreath form. The glue should run along an imaginary line that radiates from the center of the wreath out to its edge. Press the fold of one of the paper circles into the glue and hold it there for a second until the glue begins to set. (photo D)

5 Add another stripe of glue about ¼ inch (6 mm) away from the folded paper circle you just added. Press a second folded circle into the glue and hold it in place as before. Continue adding circles to the wreath form in this fashion until the entire surface is covered. (photos E and F) Repeat the process with the small wreath.

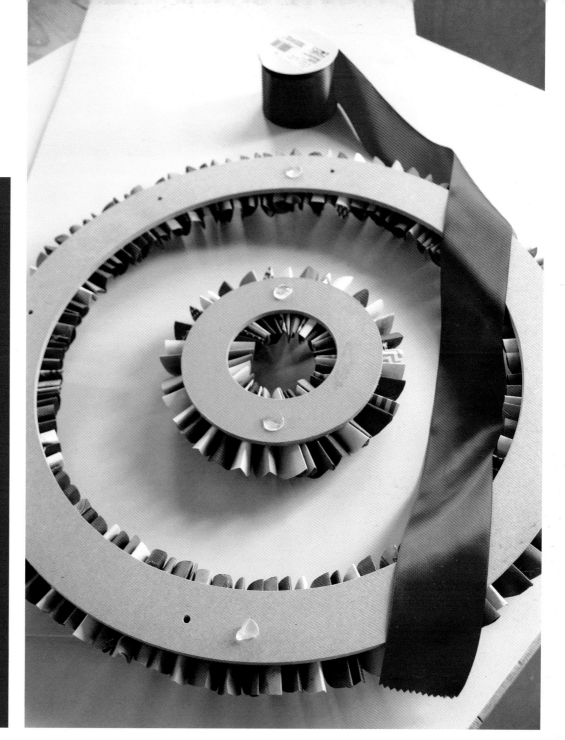

MATERIALS

craft or scrapbooking
paper in a variety of
colors and patterns

flat masonite wreath
forms, one large
(18 inches [45.7 cm])
and one small
(6 inches [15.2 cm])

1 yard (.9 m)
red satin ribbon,
2 inches (5 cm) wide

TOOLS

circle cutter or glass
to use as
circle template

scissors

glue gun

6 Combine the two wreaths into one: Lay each wreath face down, with the small wreath centered in the large one. Put a sizable dollop of hot glue on the backs of the wreaths at the top and the bottom of each as shown. Make sure the dots of glue are aligned with one another. Then press the satin ribbon into the glue, leaving plenty of excess ribbon at each end. Hold the ribbon in place until the glue begins to set. Once the glue is dry, cut off the lower end of the ribbon to a point that's about 6 inches (15.2 cm) below the bottom of the wreath. Cut it straight across or make a V-shaped cut for a more finished effect. Leave about 1½ feet (45.7 cm) of ribbon at the top of the wreath so you can tie it for hanging. (see above)

Folded Star

ORNAMENTS

A series of simple folds is all that's required to transform flat paper into a star that radiates three-dimensional splendor. Create a galaxy for your holiday tree!

MATERIALS

several sheets of patterned paper

large pearl and metal beads

metallic embroidery floss

TOOLS

scissors

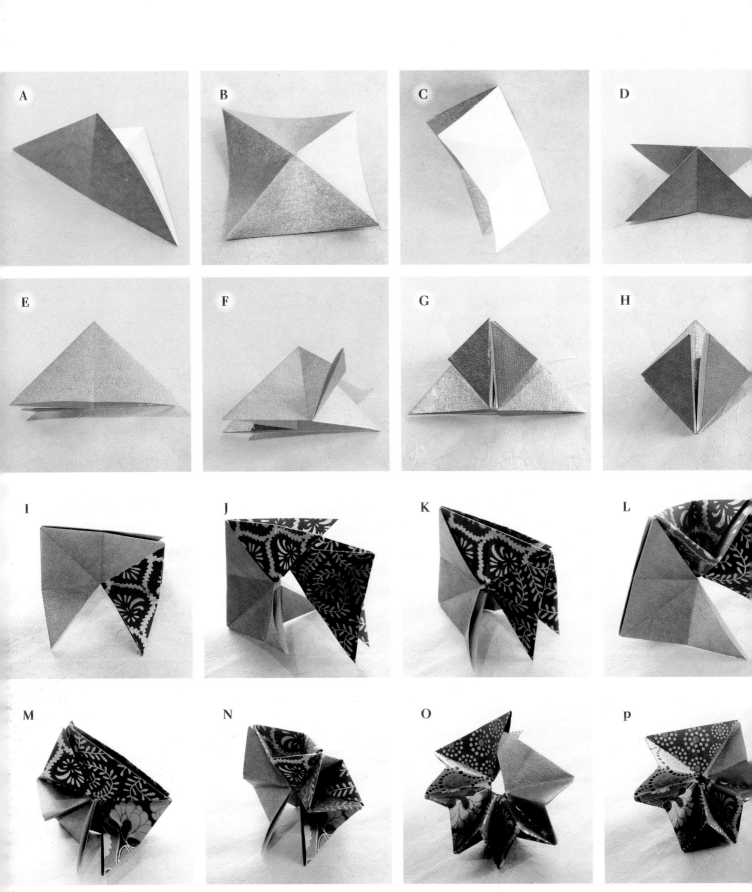

PREPARATION: Cut your paper into squares of about 4 inches (10.2 cm). You'll need six squares per star.

1 Start with one of the paper squares wrong side up. Fold it in half diagonally: Fold the bottom left corner up to meet the top right corner, crease the paper, and unfold it. Then fold the bottom right corner up to meet the top left corner. Crease the paper and unfold it. (photo A)

2 Turn the paper over so that the right side faces up. (photo B)

3 Fold the paper in half along its center. The right sides should be touching. Crease the paper and unfold it. Then fold the paper in half along its other axis. Crease it and unfold it. (photo C)

4 With the right side of the paper facing up, nudge the folds on either side inward as shown. (photo D)

5 Your paper should now be folded into a double-triangle configuration. Crease it well. (photo E)

6 Fold the right-hand point of the triangle up to the top of the triangle as shown. (photo F)

7 Fold the left-hand point of the triangle up as well. Their open edges should meet down the center as shown. (photo G) Turn the paper over, and fold the points of the triangles up on the other side. (photo H)

8 Repeat all of the steps to make 6 of these folded and creased pieces. Then gently unfold them until they're back to the folded triangle as in photo E.

9 Begin assembling the star by inserting the points of one end of the triangular piece into the folds of another piece. (photo I) Make sure the points slide in as far as possible.

10 Now insert the pointed ends of the next piece into the folds of the piece from the previous step (photo J), making sure the points go all the way in. (photo K)

11 Press down on the middle piece (the red section in the photo) to force the creases formed in step 7 to fold out. (photo L)

12 Continue to work your way around the star, adding another triangle to the mix as before. (photo M)

13 Repeat step 11 to force the creases to fold out on the next piece over. (photo N)

14 Continue adding pieces and forcing the previous creases to fold out until you have attached all six pieces of the star. Insert the points of the last triangular piece into the folds of the first piece. (photo O)

15 Work the points all the way in as far as they will go. Once they are seated deeply, press down on the first piece to force the creases to fold out as was done on all the previous pieces. The paper star is now complete. (photo P)

ADD THE EMBELLISHMENTS: The star is lovely in its unadorned state, but if you want to give it a little extra holiday bling, try this:

Thread the metallic embroidery floss through one of the large beads (I used a pearl bead). The bead should be big enough so that it can't be pulled through the center hole of the star. Tie a knot to hold the floss on the bead. Send the end of the floss through the hole in the star and pull the bead tight against the hole. Loop the floss along one of the troughs between two pieces of the star, around the back side of the star, and up again through the hole. Then loop the floss along the next trough and repeat until you've threaded each trough around the entire star. End with the embroidery floss coming up and through the hole on the side of the star that's opposite to the pearl bead. Flip the star over. Send the floss through another large bead (like the metal doughnut-shaped one shown at right), and then thread it through another pearl bead. Send the floss end back down through the metal bead and through the star's center hole, back to the side with the original pearl bead. Tie the floss end around the single pearl bead, and knot it to secure.

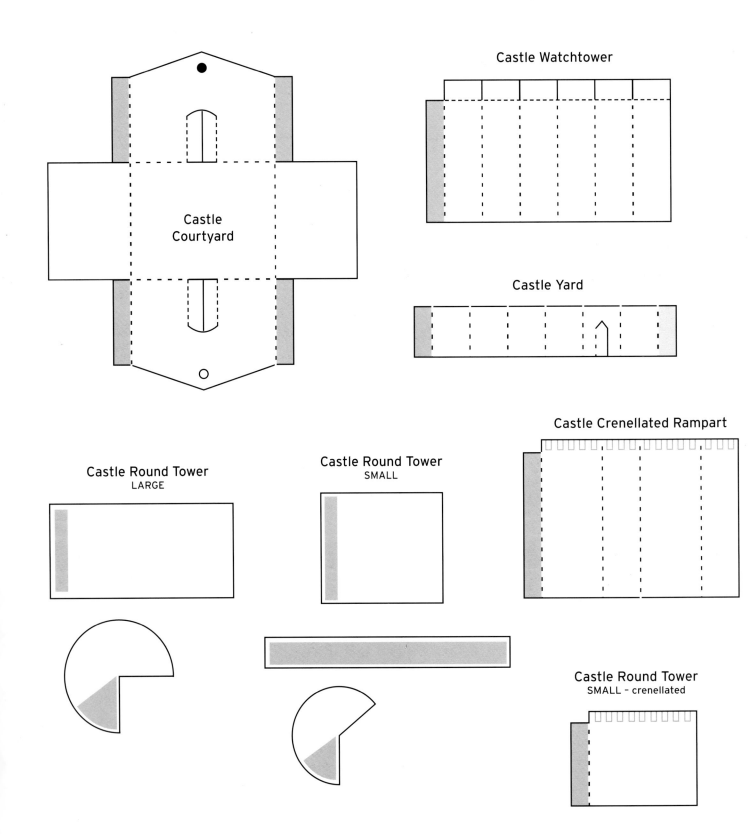

Castle Watchtower

Castle Courtyard

Castle Yard

Castle Crenellated Rampart

Castle Round Tower
LARGE

Castle Round Tower
SMALL

Castle Round Tower
SMALL – crenellated

HAPPY
CHRISTMAS

JOY!

Happy
HOLIDAYS

HO HO HO

H is for Holiday

Joy to the World

About the Author

Susan Wasinger designs houses, products, books, and magazines. Her work has been featured in *Metropolitan Home*, *Stitch*, *Natural Home*, and *Piecework* magazines, as well as on HGTV. She is the author of several books, including *Eco Craft* (Lark 2009), *The Feisty Stitcher* (Lark, 2010) and *Artful Halloween* (Lark 2012). She lives in Boulder, CO.

SODA CAN TREETOP CONE
Page 56

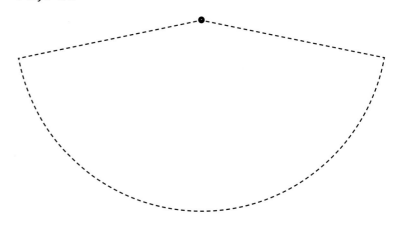

Index

Gift Wrap

Buttons & String Replace Ribbon & Bow, 68

Color-Blocked Gift Bags, 114

Wrapping Ideas From the Casbah, 66

Materials 11

Table Decorations

Doily Snowflake Bowl, 13

Faux Fortuny Chargers, 26

Folk Art Felted Coasters, 74

Glittering Castle, 86

Muslin Advent Calendar, 102

Silvered Glass Votive Holders, 110

Soda Can Punched Metal Trees, 56

Stenciled Chargers, 31

Wool-on-Linen Table Runner, 78

Techniques 8

Tools 11

Tree Decorations

Christmas Beasts for Your Tree, 52

Folded Page Snowflakes, 82

Folded Star Ornaments, 122

Marbled Ornaments, 34

Modern Graphic Felted Ornaments, 48

Plaster Relief Ornaments, 15

Playing Cards Ornaments, 43

Sand Painted Ornaments, 106

Wall Decorations

Bead Emboldened Elizabethan Wreath, 70

Cookie Cutter Garland, 95

Double Circle Wreath, 118

Plaster Relief Ornaments, 15

Pressed Clay Wreath, 20

Stockings with All the Trimmings, 38

Tiny Tin Advent Calendar Wreath, 92

Toy Catalog Vintage Glitter Garland, 22

Window Decorations

Lacy Stars Holiday Windows, 61

TRIMMED STOCKINGS
Page 38   Enlarge 300%

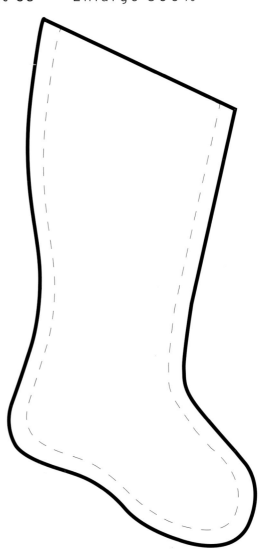